AT THE
JAPANESE TABLE

NEW AND TRADITIONAL RECIPES

BY LESLEY DOWNER

CHRONICLE BOOKS · SAN FRANCISCO

TO MY FATHER AND MOTHER

Library of Congress Cataloging in Publication Data

Downer, Lesley.
At the Japanese table : new and traditional recipes / Lesley Downer.
p.   cm.
Includes index.
ISBN 0-8118-0319-8 (pbk.)
1. Cookery, Japanese.   I. Title.
TX724.5.J3D674   1983
641.5952—dc20   92-31597
                        CIP

Design – DelRae Roth
Photography – Chris Turner
Printed in Singapore.

ISBN 0-8118-0319-8

Distributed in Canada by Raincoast Books
8680 Cambie Street
Vancouver, B.C. V6P 6M9

10 9 8 7 6 5 4 3 2

Chronicle Books
275 Fifth Street, San Francisco, CA 94103

CONTENTS

INTRODUCTION

Hajimeni

Learning about Japanese cooking is like discovering a whole new approach to food. It is also a way of getting to know an exciting and surprisingly little-known country and its culture—for Japan and its cooking are inextricably bound together.

I had my first taste of Japan and Japanese food in 1978, when I left England to live in an obscure provincial city as an English teacher. People in Japan always welcome visitors with food and in my case, as I came from a foreign country, they provided banquets to welcome me. The hospitality was amazing; but more amazing still were the dishes that appeared on the table.

In 1978 raw fish—sushi and sashimi—was still an outlandish food in England, not the fashionable dish it has become today. Yet there it was, a veritable land-scape of sashimi, complete with the still-throbbing head and tail of the fish whose flesh lay in slabs on the platter. There were trays full of glistening sushi (fish pressed on rice) and all sorts of other delicacies: soup with a carp's head floating in it (it was little comfort to be told that the head is reserved for the guest of honor); a whole grilled fish, looking at me out of a beady eye; bowls containing minute portions of different vegetables, some familiar, some not—fernheads, burdock, and horsetail shoots; and, to my relief, a basket of tem-pura—deep-fried prawns and vegetables—which seemed the least extraordinary of these extraordinary foods.

I was willing to try practically anything, except the raw fish; but my hosts pressed me just to taste it. Finally, with great reluctance, I picked up one of the gleaming red slabs with my chopsticks and put it in my mouth. It was a revela-tion—rich, succulent, flavorful, almost buttery, utterly unlike the sliminess I had been expecting.

Thence began my fascination with Japan and its food. And ever since then I have never ceased to be amazed by the variety of Japanese cuisine, its strange and wonderful new tastes, and the new ways of dealing with familiar foods.

Not All Raw Fish
varieties of Japanese cuisine

Japanese food, of course, is very far from just raw fish. It encompasses, at one end of the scale, the hautest of *hautes cuisines, kaiseki*, and at the other the delicious little dishes conjured up in tiny smoky stalls under the railway arches or along the roadside. In between comes a great variety of different sorts of food.

KAISEKI *Kaiseki* chefs are masters at creating pictures with food. When you are served a *kaiseki* meal, the first thing you do is look at it. *Kaiseki* began as dishes to go with the tea ceremony, and it consists of as many as 15 or 20 tiny dishes, some no more than a mouthful. Each one is like an exquisite work of art, served on a beautiful piece of china; and each consists of some fresh and seasonal food, often decorated with a blossom or a leaf to point up the season.

The whole notion of food as art has been a great influence on *nouvelle cuisine*. Many of the leading *nouvelle cuisine* chefs, from Paul Bocuse onwards, have been to Japan to study *kaiseki*. The influence has gone the other way too. Nowadays young Japanese chefs are creating everything from *kaiseki* French—a multitude of tiny dishes, each containing a mouthful of food cooked in the French style—to post-modern *kaiseki*, where your sashimi comes as a spectacular spotlit landscape, or the tiny jewel-like dishes laid out before you include exotic Western foods like beef, cheese, or raisins.

SPECIALTY RESTAURANTS Many of Japan's most delicious dishes are served in specialty restaurants, where the food is prepared right before your eyes. Sushi bars are rather noisy, crowded places, where you perch on a stool at the counter and watch the chef give an awesome display of his prowess with the knife while he slices and molds your raw fish. Tempura restaurants serve nothing but tempura and noodle shops nothing but noodles, which they often make on the premises. Teppanyaki, a fairly new style of cooking, is served in restaurants where each table is a gleaming stainless steel counter and the chefs perform juggling feats with their knives before cooking your meal for you.

Many fish restaurants specialize in one particular sort of fish, cooked in a hundred different ways. At a *fugu* (blowfish) restaurant, you can eat this rather alarming fish (the faintest hint of its liver can kill you) as sashimi, deep-fried in batter, simmered, or grilled; and when you call for hot sake, it comes with a piece of *fugu* fin aflame on top. Elderly Japanese men are said to be particularly fond of *fugu* fin for its aphrodisiac properties. At eel restaurants, the chefs stand in the window grilling succulent fillets of eel over charcoal and your meal includes eel liver soup, skewered and grilled eel heads, and deep-fried eel backbone. There are also restaurants specializing in different varieties of wild mushrooms and wild plants from the mountains.

"RED LANTERNS" AND STREET FOOD Some of Japan's best food is to be found in little street stalls or in the drinking houses with red lanterns hanging outside where office workers gather of an evening before starting on the long commute home. These drinking houses specialize in home cooking, "just like mother makes": small bowls of salad or simmered vegetables, raw bonito fish mixed with spring onion, or fish and vegetables skewered and grilled over charcoal. Some—no more than a hut, hardly big enough for six customers—serve *yakitori*, chicken kebabs brushed with a sweet thick sauce. Others serve deep-fried vegetables on skewers. Around railway stations you can find small carts which incorporate a charcoal stove and also have a red lantern hanging up. These dispense plebeian but satisfying dishes like *oden*, chunks of assorted vegetables and fish simmered in sweet stock, or big bowls of noodles or grilled octopus.

TEMPLE COOKING Until a hundred years ago, the Japanese followed the tenets of Buddhism and ate no meat. Even today, most people eat more fish and less meat than we do; and there are Buddhist temples that have small restaurants on the premises, serving vegetarian food. Many of these dishes are based on tofu and other soybean products. Some are simple dishes such as those cooked by families at home—simmering tofu in winter, chilled tofu in summer. Others magically transform the white curd into unusual and wonderful dishes.

Home Cooking
the bedrock of Japanese cuisine
■

Kaiseki is the pinnacle of Japanese cuisine, but home cooking is its bedrock. Day after day, in millions of kitchens all over Japan, rice bubbles in electric rice cookers and mothers labor to produce food just as their mothers made it. For, despite the advent of McDonalds, sending out for pizzas, and frozen fish fingers, the Japanese continue to eat Japanese food. Of course, like everything else in Japan, food changes with the times. Mothers now have to cook two meals each evening—fish fingers for the children and a traditional meal for the grandparents. And the Japanese themselves are changing. The younger generation, brought up on a diet that includes beef and milk, are noticeably taller and larger than their parents.

RICE The basis of nearly every meal is rice—Japanese rice, pure white and gleaming. For breakfast, lunch, and dinner, the rice cooker is carried into the dining room and set down on the floor beside the table. When everyone has had their fill of the small dishes that crowd the table, the mother of the family opens the rice cooker and ladles out bowl after bowl of steaming rice. Just as wheat was once a staple for much of Europe and America in the past, rice is still very much so for the Japanese. No matter how many other dishes you eat, you will not feel that you have really eaten until you have had rice. Rice is always served plain—it would never do to put soy sauce on it—with pickled vegetables and miso soup to go with it.

Harvesting Land and Sea
the range of ingredients
■

When you travel in Japan, you see immediately the importance of rice. The countryside is a patchwork of paddy fields and there are paddies cut into every available space. Steep mountain shelves are carved into steps for rice growing, and there are even paddies between houses in the suburbs of Tokyo. In the same way, the land determines the range of ingredients that Japanese cooks use.

Japan is made up of islands, a good half of which are taken up with mountains and forest, and the remaining half with cities, factories, and rice fields. There is very little space left for vegetable growing, let alone grazing.

VEGETABLES As a result of the lack of space, the Japanese have become very resourceful. Besides cultivated vegetables they also use wild ones, gathered from the mountains—a variety of wild mushrooms in the autumn, and roots, shoots, stalks, and leaves in the spring. Many edible plants that the rest of the world is just rediscovering are on sale in every market and supermarket in Japan, such as burdock, fernheads, butterbur, and mountain celery. In remote parts of the country they still eat insects—locusts and bee larvae—though this seems as outlandish to the average Tokyoite as it does to us. (There are no insect recipes in this book!)

MEAT Apart from the northern island, Hokkaido, where the climate is more temperate, there is very little pastureland in Japan. Beef cattle live out their lives, rather sadly, in sheds. The most fortunate are those likely to yield the best beef. They are kept underground or in ranches around Kobe, and enjoy plenty of beer and a daily massage to smooth the fat evenly through their muscles. The result is marbled Kobe or Matsuzaka beef, the most prized and expensive in the world.

The raising of beef cattle is a recent development in Japan. Until 100 years ago, the Japanese ate no meat, and fish is still a central part of the Japanese diet. Almost every Japanese meal includes fish, and some consist entirely of fish.

FISH The Japanese are a nation of islanders, and they know how to make full use of the produce of the rivers and the sea. The variety of fish and seafoods in the average Japanese fishmonger's is quite astonishing. Every morning at dawn, Tokyo fishmongers go along to the great fish market, Tsukiji, where lorries are just rolling in, laden with fresh fish and seafood straight from the coast. Much of the fish is so fresh that it is still alive. There are tanks full of wriggling eels and splashing fish. One of Tokyo's great sights is the daily tuna auction, at five o'clock in the morning, when fishmongers bid for chunks of the great red fish.

SEAWEEDS Another very important product of the sea is seaweed, rich in iodine and minerals. The Japanese do not simply gather seaweed but cultivate it. Kombu (kelp), the basis for dashi and one of the most important flavors of Japanese cuisine, comes from the cold waters of Hokkaido. Nori (laver) is cultivated in the warmer waters of Kyushu and dried like paper on bamboo frames.

Despite the advent of imported unseasonal foods, most housewives still shop daily and rely largely on fresh local seasonal produce. In a market or the food section of a department store in Japan, the variety and quality of food on display is astonishing. The vegetables are glossy, sparkling (salad vegetables are continually sprinkled with water), and perfectly shaped; the fish either still alive or fresh from the ocean, lustrous and bright-eyed.

The Distinctive Flavors

■

With ingredients of such quality, overcooking or heavy-handed seasoning would be a positive crime. Most food is cooked simply and lightly. In fact, the very best ingredients are served raw, as sashimi, with just a touch of soy sauce and wasabi to point up the flavor; beef, as well as fish, can be served this way.

As a result, Japanese food tastes distinctively clean and fresh. The stars of the show are the ingredients themselves; and they are often cooked separately, rather than mixed together, so that each taste remains pure. The various flavorings and seasonings serve to complement the ingredients rather than to change them, spice them up or mask them in heavy sauces.

The main flavoring elements are mild and delicate, and derive from the same natural environment as the ingredients. Dashi, the basic stock that puts in an appearance in nearly every dish and provides the underlying flavor for soups and simmered foods, comes from the sea. It is made from kombu (kelp) and dried shavings of the bonito fish.

Other key flavors are from the land—from rice, which grows across so much of the country, and from soybeans. Rice is the source of sake, a rich sweet wine that is splashed liberally into every dish, like wine in French cooking. Mirin, a delicate cooking wine, is also made from rice, as is the sweet mild vinegar used in salads and to make sushi.

From soybeans comes soy sauce, one of the most important flavors in Japanese cookery—lighter and milder than Chinese soy sauce. Soybeans are also the source of the more earthy and powerful flavors, like miso, a salty paste made from fermented soybeans, used daily for miso soup.

A Healthy Diet

■

Not surprisingly, many of these ingredients have found their way onto the shelves of our health food shops. Japanese food is some of the healthiest there is, low in high-cholesterol items like red meat, dairy products, and saturated oils, and high in seafoods and seaweeds, which are full of minerals. As evidence of their good health, Japanese have a longer lifespan than any other nation on earth, and a startlingly low incidence of heart disease. Conversely, they have a rather high level of salt-related diseases—their diet contains a lot of salty items like soy sauce and miso. However, little by little this general high level of health is dropping off, as the younger generation switches to a more westernized diet of milk, hamburgers, and sugary foods.

A Visual Feast

■

Japanese food is marvelously light and simply flavored, relying heavily on the quality of the ingredients themselves—an art, in fact, which is reassuringly simple to learn. What differentiates the professional chef from the home cook is not so much his skill in mixing flavors as his artistry.

Watching the master chef at work is rather like watching Picasso putting the finishing touches to a painting or, to put it in a Japanese context, a master arranging flowers and branches in a vase. In Nadaman, one of Tokyo's top *kaiseki* restaurants, I have watched while the master chef arranges paper-thin slices of raw turbot with infinite care into a white "chrysanthemum," adds a couple of dark-purple *shiso* leaves, stands back, tilts his head to study the effect, ponders, makes a minute adjustment, steps back again and nods with satisfaction. His palette is food, and what he is creating is a work of art designed to please both the eye and the tongue.

This perspective on food and its possibilities in not limited to *kaiseki* chefs. The great distinguishing feature of Japanese cuisine, from *kaiseki* down to the humblest noodle restaurant or the simplest home meal, is that it is a decorative art. Home cooks as well as *kaiseki* chefs arrange each dish as beautifully as possible, so that looking at it can be as pleasurable an experience as eating it.

The Four Seasons

The dishes on Japanese tables change through the year. The Japanese are acutely aware of the passing of the four seasons and love to celebrate them.

In spring, when the cherry blossom comes out, people go on expeditions to admire the best and most beautiful trees, and sit under the spreading branches, drinking sake or beer and eating elaborate packed lunches, while the pink blossom drifts down like snow. The appearance of the blossoms is such an event that it is always greeted with headlines in the national papers. This is the season of fresh young leaves and shoots, as well as fish—young bamboo shoots, wild foods from the mountains, and young trout and bonito. To underline the season, there are always blossoms or tiny brilliant green leaves decorating each dish.

Summer is hot and sultry, the season for oily foods like eggplant and eel, which are supposed to give you energy (there is actually one particular day in July, officially the hottest day of summer, that is eel-eating day when everyone dutifully eats eel). There is iced tea, iced noodles and tofu on ice, and fresh green soybeans.

Autumn is the time for wild mushrooms, chestnuts, pumpkin, and sweet potatoes, and each dish is decorated with tiny red and gold maple leaves. While people avoid raw fish in summer—the heat is such that it can spoil very quickly—in autumn plenty of fish are at their best.

Winter is the season for crab, blowfish, and thick warming stews cooked at table, when everyone sits around helping themselves to piping-hot food from the pot.

The Structure of a Japanese Meal

■

There is no "meat and two veg" in a Japanese meal. In fact, when Japanese eat Western food they tend to complain about the size of the portions and the lack of variety. Japanese food is served in tiny delicate portions, each item carefully arranged on its own small plate and garnished. Each food is fresh and seasonal and quite perfect, chosen as much for its color and shape as for its flavor.

As in Chinese cuisine, the balance of the meal depends on the actual cooking methods used. The basis of nearly every meal is rice, pickles, and miso soup. These form a meal in themselves and also provide the coda for the more complex meals.

"SOUP PLUS THREE" The simplest meal cooked at home consists of three dishes cooked by different methods—most commonly sashimi (raw fish), a grilled dish, and a simmered dish—followed by rice and soup, making up "soup plus three."

A KAISEKI MEAL At the other end of the scale, a *kaiseki* meal provides a sample of every cooking technique in the Japanese repertoire. While home-cooked meals are served all at once, the dishes in a *kaiseki* meal are served one by one in a specific order—the order of the recipes in this book. When you visit a *kaiseki* restaurant, you never know exactly what dishes you will be served. The menu does not give details of the contents of each dish, but only the cooking method: first appetizers, then a clear soup, then sashimi, followed by a grilled dish, a simmered dish, a deep-fried dish, a steamed dish, and a salad, in that order. Finally, marking the end of the meal, rice, served with pickles and miso soup. The actual ingredients of each dish vary day by day, depending on what is fresh and in season.

Serving Japanese Food at Home

There is no need to begin your adventures in Japanese food by cooking a whole meal. Individual Japanese dishes fit well into a Western meal; you could serve them as side dishes or as small dishes at a party, for example.

When you come to plan a full Japanese meal, the crucial considerations are variety and balance. Choose recipes using different cooking techniques—a "soup plus three" might be a good way to begin. Make sure that the meal includes a balance of fish and vegetable dishes and that the ingredients and recipes are appropriate for the season. And keep in mind the visual appearance of each dish.

There is no dessert in a traditional Japanese meal. Sometimes fresh fruit is offered, beautifully carved, and sweet cakes are often served at tea time.

Another aspect of Japanese food is that it is rarely served hot, and is usually eaten at room temperature, when the flavors can be best appreciated. There is no need to reheat a dish put to one side while you finish off another.

Food for the Eye

Even the simplest Japanese dish is composed a little like a picture. From the very beginning, the cook considers the visual possibilities of the food as well as its taste.

PERFECT SEASONAL FOOD The ingredients you choose should be fresh, seasonal, and as perfect as possible. Japanese shopkeepers usually give away knobbly strawberries, for example, because nobody will buy them. You will need foods of different colors and shapes, and some that can be used as garnishes.

CUTTING TECHNIQUES The Japanese lay great store by the cutting of different ingredients; in fact, one mark of a great chef is his prowess with the knife. Each ingredient has to be cut quite carefully, sometimes into small pieces so that it will cook more easily, sometimes simply to make it look more beautiful. Many vegetables are decoratively cut to add to the beauty of the dish.

COOKING CONSERVATIVELY Many Japanese cooking techniques are designed to preserve and enhance the shape and color of the food. Fish are skewered so that they will keep their shape while they are grilled. Green vegetables are cooked for only a few seconds, then rinsed in cold water to retain their color.

PLATES AND DISHES The plate is as much a part of the picture as the food that goes onto it. The plates in a Japanese kitchen are usually small and of every imaginable shape, and the choice of the right dishes to go with the food and the season is an important part of the preparation of the meal. Choose dishes to complement the food in both shape and color (see Tableware pages 34–5).

ARRANGING FOOD IN THE DISH The first mark of a great chef is his skill with the knife; the second is the artistry with which he arranges food in the dish. The actual quantities of food in each dish are usually small.

Food is always carefully arranged; it should not fill the whole dish but be artistically placed in the center. Salad is served in a mound in the middle of the bowl, not touching the edges. Simmered foods are arranged like a landscape painting, with larger items like mountains in the background and smaller ones in front. Grilled fish are served on flat, rectangular plates, with the head facing to the left. Most dishes are garnished with a leaf or carved vegetable, which gives a contrast of taste, color, or shape, and which is also a pleasing reminder of the season.

ARRANGING DISHES ON THE TABLE When setting the table, the cardinal rule is that all the dishes in each place setting should be different. At each place there will be a pair of chopsticks on a chopstick rest. For an informal meal, the placing of dishes is fairly arbitrary; a Japanese table is usually crammed with tiny plates and dishes. When, at the end of the meal, you serve the rice and soup, rice goes to the left and soup to the right, in front of the other dishes. If you serve large communal dishes of food, you should also provide serving chopsticks.

Eating with Chopsticks

■

Japanese food is designed to be eaten with chopsticks and tastes much better that way. The notion of bringing a weapon like a knife to table is quite barbaric in Japanese eyes! Most food is served in bite-sized pieces and larger items, like eggplants, are well cooked so that they can be eased apart with chopsticks.

USING CHOPSTICKS Using chopsticks is a knack that is quite easy to master. First pick up one chopstick and hold it between the thumb and first two fingers of your hand, like a pencil; this is the chopstick that will move. Put the second chopstick between your second and third fingers and behind your thumb; this one stays still. Move the top chopstick up and down with your thumb and first finger.

It is perfectly acceptable in Japan to pick up a bowl of rice or food while you are eating from it.

1 Both chopsticks in position.

2 Move the top chopstick up and down.

Tea and Sake

■

Japanese food can be served with tea, sake, beer, whiskey, or wine.

TEA Japanese tea is green. It is made from the same tea plants as Indian tea, but instead of being fermented, it is simply dried, and retains a lovely refreshing delicate flavor. There are many different grades of Japanese tea. The coarsest, *bancha,* is made of twigs and stems as well as leaves. *Sencha* is a finer tea, made from top-quality leaves.

Japanese tea is made not with boiling water but with water just a little hotter than drinking temperature. It should be poured out straight away, not left to steep.

SAKE Sake is literally the drink of the gods. There are always rows of sake casks in front of Shinto shrines, donated by petitioners. It is made from rice, steamed, fermented, and mixed with pure water. In winter there is nothing better than hot sake out of tiny cups the size of egg cups, and in summer cold sake, drunk from small, square, wooden mugs.

Sake has no vintage; it is best drunk young, within three months of being bottled or at the longest within the year. Budding sake buffs should focus instead on where it comes from. Sake made in Nada, near Kobe, is said to be "masculine," clean and vigorous in taste, while Fushimi, near Kyoto, produces a more delicate, "feminine" sake. Akita in the north and Hiroshima in the south also produce fine sake. To the connoisseur, only *junmaishu*—prime sake, unadulterated with added alcohol or sugar—is worth considering. Connoisseurs also prefer dry sake, though restaurants nearly always serve sweet. There are three grades of sake: *tokkyu* (special), *ikkyu* (first grade), and *nikyu* (second grade).

When you drink sake, you should always fill everyone else's cup but not your own. As you raise your glass, you shout "*Kampai!*"—"Bottoms up!"

INGREDIENTS
AND EQUIPMENT

Zairyo to Dogu

Ingredients

ZAIRYO

■

One of the most exciting things about Japanese cooking is getting acquainted with a whole new palate of ingredients. It is not strictly essential to use Japanese ingredients; there are substitutes for many. But to ensure a really authentic taste, it's worth seeking out some of the basic items. The two key ingredients are dashi, stock made with bonito flakes and kombu seaweed, and Japanese soy sauce, which is completely different from the Chinese varieties.

As Japanese cookery becomes better known, more and more ordinary grocers and supermarkets are stocking Japanese items. Some of the items listed below you will find in your local supermarket and some in health food shops or delicatessens; for others you will have to go to a Japanese specialty grocery or other Asian markets. Finally, if you can't find some items locally, they most likely can be ordered by mail. (See Mail-Order Sources on page 220.)

BONITO FLAKES, DRIED *Katsuo-Bushi* The bonito fish is a relative of the mackerel and tuna. It is filleted and dried until it is rock hard and then shaved into wispy aromatic flakes, which are used to make dashi and as a garnish. Freshly shaved bonito flakes have a wonderful smoky aroma and are the most delicious, but they also come ready-flaked. Bonito flakes are sold by the packet in Japanese groceries and some supermarkets. For dashi, the smallest, cheapest flakes are fine, and are sold in bags of 0.175 ounce each, in packs of 5 bags. When used as a garnish, large feathery shavings are tastier than small ones.

DAIKON RADISH This is also sold as Japanese radish, or Chinese turnip. It looks rather like a large white carrot and is widely available in shops and markets selling exotic vegetables. It is supposed to have no calories and to be a great digestive, and is always served grated raw with deep-fried dishes like tempura to counter-act the oiliness. Look for firm, white, unwrinkled daikon.

To grate daikon, use a Japanese grater (see page 33) or any fine-toothed standard grater. Allow the juices to drain away, then squeeze the daikon, either with your fingers or through muslin, and shape it into a small mound.

DASHI Dashi is Japanese stock—the basic stock that provides the underlying flavor for most Japanese dishes. It is made from dried bonito fish flakes and kombu seaweed and has a very distinctive and lovely smell of the sea.

In the old days, everyone always made their dashi from scratch. The best dashi is still homemade, but nowadays most Japanese housewives rely on instant dashi. There are several excellent instant dashi powders available, which have a very authentic flavor. Simply mix with enough water to make a delicately flavored stock. Ask for *dashi-no-moto* or *hon-dashi* in Japanese grocery stores and some supermarkets. (Note for the health-conscious: check the list of ingredients before you buy instant dashi; some brands contain monosodium glutamate.)

If you are planning to make only one or two Japanese dishes, it is more convenient to use instant dashi. But if you are planning a whole Japanese meal, it is sensible to begin by making a large batch of fresh dashi. There are two grades, Dashi I and Dashi II. Dashi II is by far the more useful for general purposes—simmering, sauces, thick soups, etc. Dashi I is much lighter and more delicate in flavor, and is used for making the beautiful clear soups that begin a classic meal.

If you don't have the ingredients for dashi at hand, don't despair. A very light chicken or vegetable stock will do well as a substitute. The dish may not be totally authentic, but it will still taste good. But to experience the true Japanese flavor, you will have to use real dashi

Unless Dashi I is specified in the recipe, use either instant dashi or Dashi II.

Dashi I

ICHIBAN DASHI

∎

MAKES 5 CUPS

1 piece (4-6 inches) dried kombu, wiped

2-3 packets (0.175 ounce each) dried bonito flakes

TO COOK Put 5 cups cold water into a large saucepan, add the kombu and heat slowly, skimming off any scum that forms on the surface. Just before the water boils, remove the kombu. Raise the heat and just as the water starts to boil again, throw in the bonito flakes. Bring to a full boil, then immediately remove the pan from the heat and allow the flakes to settle. Strain gently through muslin (do not squeeze).

Dashi II

NIBAN DASHI

■

MAKES ABOUT 5 CUPS

1 piece (4-6 inches) dried kombu, wiped

3-5 packets (0.175 ounce each) dried bonito flakes

TO COOK Put the kombu into 7½ cups cold water and bring to a simmer (do not boil kombu as this makes it bitter). Skim off any scum that forms. Add 2 or 3 packets of the bonito flakes and simmer uncovered for about 20 minutes, until the stock is well reduced. Toss in another 1 or 2 packets of bonito and immediately remove from the heat. Allow the flakes to settle, then strain.

Alternatively, reserve the kombu and bonito flakes used in Dashi I and simmer them in 3 quarts water for 20 minutes; finally add 1 or 2 packets of bonito flakes, strain and use.

TO STORE Dashi I should always be freshly made, but Dashi II can be stored in a sealed bottle in the refrigerator for up to 3 days or can be frozen; however, flavor and aroma will be lost.

GINGER *Shoga* Fresh ginger root is an essential ingredient in the Japanese kitchen. Its sweetly pungent taste adds a lift to many dishes and it is also valued for its digestive properties. Dried ginger is not a substitute. Select firm unshriveled ginger roots and peel away the brown skin before use. Grate with a Japanese grater (see page 33) or any fine-toothed grater.

Ginger juice is made by squeezing finely grated ginger, either with your fingers or through muslin.

Red pickled ginger, to accompany sushi, is sold by the packet in Japanese grocery stores as *gari* or *beni-shoga*.

GINGKO NUTS *Ginnan* Gingko nuts have a wonderfully delicate flavor and texture and are well worth seeking out. They are available canned in specialty food shops and very occasionally fresh, in the autumn. To prepare fresh gingko nuts, first crack the outer shell with a nutcracker and remove, then soak the nuts in hot water for a few minutes and rub away the inner skin.

GOURD STRIPS *Kampyo* These long white ribbonlike strips are carved from the edible gourd and used as a sort of vegetable string or in simmered dishes. They are sold dried, by the packet, in Japanese grocery stores (they may be labeled "dried gourd shavings") and need to be softened before use. Stored in an airtight canister, they keep indefinitely.

To prepare gourd strips separate out the required amount of strips, put them into a bowl and knead with plenty of salt to soften the fibers. Rinse well and soak in lukewarm water for a few minutes, then simmer according to the recipe.

HARUSAME NOODLES *Harusame* —"spring rain" noodles—are very fine, translucent white noodles made from rice or potato flour. They are sold in Japanese grocery stores in 5-ounce packs as "Japanese saifun."

HIJIKI SEAWEED One of the tastiest seaweeds, hijiki really deserves the appellation "sea vegetable." It is black, stringy, sweet, and rather chewy and is supposed to be full of vital iodine and minerals. It makes a very tasty addition to mixed vegetable dishes and can be found in health food shops as well as Japanese grocery stores. There is no need to soak before using. Stored in an airtight canister, hijiki will keep indefinitely.

KOMBU SEAWEED This is kelp, dried to make long dark-green or brown leathery strands. It is an essential ingredient for dashi and is also eaten as a vegetable; like all seaweeds, it is very rich in minerals. Before use, it should be lightly wiped; some Japanese chefs score the surface to bring out the flavor. The easiest way to cut it is with scissors. Kombu is liable to become bitter and should always be simmered rather than boiled. It is sold in health food shops and Japanese grocery stores, and will keep indefinitely stored in an airtight canister. Occasionally in Japanese food stores you will find it labeled "tangle" rather than kombu.

KONNYAKU This jellylike, pearly gray cake is made from the root of a sort of sweet potato. It has a bland, slightly fishy flavor—an acquired taste, but one worth acquiring. It is an important ingredient in many cooked dishes and salads and is supposed to have no calories at all and to be very good for the digestion. Stored under water it will keep for 2 weeks and should be dry-roasted or par-boiled before using. (You may find it labeled "boiled yam cake.")

KUZU STARCH Kuzu is the king of thickeners. A delicate powder made from the root of the kuzu vine, it gives a particularly light and translucent quality to soups and sauces and makes a light crisp coating for fried foods. In Japan it is also valued for its medicinal properties. Kuzu is sold in health food shops as well as Japanese grocery stores (you may find it labeled "arum root powder"); cornstarch and arrowroot are acceptable substitutes.

Kuzu comes in hard rocklike lumps. Before using, it should be ground to a powder. This is easiest of all using a *suribachi*—a Japanese mortar and pestle (see page 34); otherwise an ordinary mortar and pestle will do.

MIRIN This sweet golden rice wine is used only for cooking, and is an essential item in the Japanese kitchen. It is sold in all Japanese groceries and some large supermarkets. If you can't find it, substitute 1 teaspoon sugar for each tablespoon mirin. Or you can just use sake instead or simply omit the mirin altogether.

MISO Some of Japan's most inspired culinary products are made from soybeans, and miso is one of them. It is a rich, savory paste made by fermenting cooked soybeans with *koji,* a yeastlike mold, and then leaving them for at least 6 months and as long as 3 years to mature. Most Japanese still have miso, in the form of miso soup, for breakfast every day; and it is used for salads, marinades, and as a spread and pickling agent. Miso comes in many varieties, thicknesses, and colors. Lighter miso is used in sauces and pale Kansai-style miso soups, and the thicker red miso for richer soups and stews and general cooking. Miso is available in health food shops as well as Japanese specialty stores. It is a very nutritious food, full of living enzymes, and should be stored in the refrigerator.

MUSHROOMS In Japan, as in France, mushrooms are not just mushrooms. There are infinite varieties and mushrooms special to particular areas of the country, including delicious wild varieties. Various types of Japanese mushrooms are becoming increasingly available in North America. Look for them, fresh or dried, in Asian markets and specialty produce shops. In most recipes, ordinary flat or button mushrooms make an acceptable substitute. See also shiitake mushrooms.

NORI SEAWEED Nori is one of the most familiar seaweeds, to be found wrapping sushi or laid out with the morning rice at breakfast time. It is actually the same as the seaweed called laver. In Japan it is farmed in the shallows around the southern island, Kyushu, and stretched on bamboo frames, like paper, to dry. It comes in many different varieties, colors, and sizes and is sold in health food shops and Japanese groceries. For the recipes in this book, buy the large 7 × 8-inch paper-thin sheets. Stored in an airtight canister, nori will keep indefinitely.

To toast nori, which should also be done before use, wave it over a hot flame for a few seconds, until it changes color and smells fragrant. Be careful—it burns very easily! Then cut it with scissors to the desired size.

OILS In Japan pure vegetable oil is used for frying and deep-frying, never butter or animal fats. Light oils like sunflower or safflower are best; corn and olive oil are too heavy. A little sesame oil is often added to the basic oil as a flavoring; for more, see sesame oil.

PICKLES *Tsukemono* Preserved vegetables are to the Japanese rather as cheese is to the French. The variety is endless. Each region produces its own specialties, which visitors to the area buy as souvenirs. At the end of a Japanese meal, pickles are *de rigeur,* as a crunchy, spicy contrast to the blandness of rice. Almost any vegetable can be pickled. The most popular include daikon radish, eggplant, Chinese cabbage, and cucumber, pickled with rice bran or salt (the most common methods), or vinegar or miso. Japanese grocers all stock a large variety of ready-made pickles. Buy two or three different sorts—select different colors and shapes—and arrange a few slices of each in a small decorative dish to serve. Keep the opened packets in the refrigerator.

POTATO FLOUR OR POTATO STARCH *Katakuriko* This is used as a thickener and an alternative to kuzu in Japanese cooking. Use cornstarch as a substitute.

RICE CAKE *Mochi* Rather like turkey in the West, rice cake goes with festive occasions. It is made by pounding glutinous rice, traditionally in a large mortar, though nowadays it is usually made by machine. The result is a chewy white cake, which is shaped into balls or squares. Commercially produced rice cakes are sold by Japanese grocers in hard dried squares. Besides being used for *ozoni,* New Year's soup, they can be grilled and eaten as a snack.

SAKE Sake is the drink of the gods in Japan. It is a marvelous alcoholic beverage made from rice, which is steamed, fermented, and refined to produce a clear limpid liquid. Like wine, different regions produce different sakes; it is said that the finest sake comes from Nada and Fushimi in central Japan, and Akita in the north. Sake is an essential ingredient in Japanese cooking, used for marinating and tenderizing food as well as for flavoring. It is sold in huge bottles, in Japanese grocery stores, and in many supermarkets and liquor stores. Dry sherry is a possible substitute, though the flavor is rather different. Sake is also, of course, the best possible accompaniment for a Japanese meal, and should be served heated in small flasks.

SESAME OIL This is a thick, rich, golden oil made from sesame seeds, with a delicious nutty flavor and aroma. It tends to burn easily and is used as a flavoring rather than a cooking oil. It is often added to flavor oil for deep frying. Japanese sesame oil is purer than Chinese and is sold by the bottle in Japanese grocery stores.

SESAME SEEDS Sesame seeds are a popular flavoring and garnish in Japanese cooking. White sesame seeds are sold in most groceries and black—which have a slightly stronger flavor—in Japanese food shops. Before use, they need to be lightly toasted to bring out the flavor.

To toast sesame seeds, heat them in a 300°F oven or in a dry frying pan until they turn golden and smell nutty. Shake the pan frequently to make sure they don't burn. The Japanese have a small pan specifically for toasting sesame seeds, with holes in the lid to stop the seeds from jumping out, but an ordinary frying pan will do.

Sesame seeds can also be ground. At first they become flaky, then, after much grinding, become oily and turn into sesame paste or tahini. Grind them in a *suribachi* (see page 34), mortar and pestle, or food processor; or use the same quantity of commercially available tahini or sesame paste.

SEVEN SPICE PEPPER *Shichimi Togarashi* This spicy condiment is a mixture of chili pepper, black pepper, ground orange peel, sesame seeds, poppy seeds, hemp seeds, and powdered nori. It is sold in Japanese grocery stores.

SHIITAKE MUSHROOMS Shiitake are the most common Japanese mushrooms. They are firmer, chewier, and more flavorful than our cultivated mushrooms and are used both fresh and dried. FRESH SHIITAKE are sold in some Asian and Japanese grocery stores as well as many supermarkets. Choose firm fleshy mushrooms with a good smell; cut off and discard the stems before use. DRIED SHIITAKE have a more intense flavor; they are sold in most Asian groceries, and keep indefinitely stored in a dry place. Before use, they need to be soaked for at least half an hour. Cut off the hard stalk, drain the mushrooms, and keep the soaking liquid, which makes a delicious stock.

SHIRATAKI Shirataki ("white waterfall") is strings of white *konnyaku,* used in sukiyaki, other dishes cooked at table, and salads. Also called "yam noodles," it is sold canned and in water packs in Japanese grocery stores. It should be rinsed, drained, and parboiled for 1 or 2 minutes before using.

SOBA NOODLES These narrow, flat, grayish-brown buckwheat noodles are sold dried in health food shops and fresh or dried at Japanese groceries.

SOMEN NOODLES These are thin white wheat noodles, usually served chilled in summer. They are sold dried in Japanese and some Chinese grocery stores.

SOY SAUCE Along with dashi, soy sauce is one of the key flavors that make Japanese food what it is. It is made by mixing together soybeans, wheat, and salt, then leaving the mixture to ferment for a year and finally pressing it to give off the dark, pungent, salty liquid. Japanese and Chinese soy sauces are quite different. The Japanese variety is sweeter and lighter; always use it for Japanese cooking.

Japanese soy sauces are graded into light and dark. Dark soy sauce is best for general cooking. Light soy sauce is paler and a little stronger, and is used for aesthetic purposes, to avoid darkening a light-colored dish. Unless light soy sauce is specified, use dark; and if you have no light soy sauce, use dark Japanese (never Chinese) soy sauce as a substitute.

TEA Japanese tea is green, made with the green unfermented leaves of the tea plant. It has a sweetish, delicate flavor, quite unlike Chinese or Indian tea, and makes a fine accompaniment to a Japanese meal. There are many grades, of which the best quality is the powdered green variety used for the tea ceremony. Japanese tea is made with water that is hot but not boiling, and should never be left to steep. Store it in an airtight canister. For more, see page 19.

TOFU (BEAN CURD) This is a wonderfully nutritious food that contains all the protein of the soybean in a very digestible form. It is made by pulping cooked soybeans, straining out the soy milk, then coagulating and pressing it in a process very similar to making cottage cheese. Although rather bland, it has the marvelous property of absorbing other flavors. Fresh tofu is sold in both firm and soft varieties at health food stores, Japanese and Chinese groceries, and many supermarkets. For the recipes in this book, use the firm type, although the more finely textured soft variety may be substituted. Tofu will keep for 4 to 5 days if stored under water in the refrigerator; make sure the tofu is completely covered with water and change the water every day.

Deep-fried tofu (*aburage*) is sold ready-made in Japanese shops. It can be pulled apart to make small sacks, which are then stuffed with vegetables or rice.

UDON NOODLES These fat, white wheat noodles, particularly popular in southern Japan, are available fresh or dried at Japanese groceries.

VINEGAR The best vinegar for Japanese cooking is Japanese rice vinegar, made from rice and much lighter, sweeter, and milder than wine, cider, or malt vinegars. If unavailable, use cider vinegar diluted with water.

WAKAME SEAWEED This nutritious seaweed with long green fronds and a silky texture is said to be particularly good for the hair and skin. It is used in soups and salads and needs very little cooking. There are many different varieties and sizes. Occasionally it comes with a tough spine, which needs to be cut off after soaking.

WASABI This is the stingingly hot, bright-green substance that lurks between the fish and the rice in sushi and brings tears to the eyes. In sushi bars it is actually called *namida*, "tears"! It is a small green root rather like a ginger root, which is grated. In the West, fresh wasabi is practically unavailable. But you can buy it powdered (mix with water, exactly like mustard) or ready-made, by the tube, in Asian grocery stores. Powdered is usually better. (You may find it labeled "Japanese horseradish," though it has nothing to do with horseradish.) Use sparingly!

A Note on Raw Ingredients

■

When most people think of Japanese food, they think of raw foods, and especially of raw fish, the most famous of all Japanese ingredients. But beware! If you are planning to try raw fish in sushi or sashimi, it is essential—for health and safety as well as flavor—that the fish be top quality and really fresh. First, be absolutely sure that the fish comes from a reliable source; find a good fish market and stick with it. Secondly, double check that the fish is superfresh. Yesterday's fish will *not* do. It must be fresh this morning. To be safe, it is best to buy the fish from a Japanese food shop, if you are lucky enough to live near one.

Similarly, many traditional Japanese recipes contain raw or very lightly cooked eggs. Before eating eggs raw, be sure that they are from a reliable source. Many health authorities also advise that persons who are at high risk of bacterial infection refrain from eating raw or soft-cooked eggs. These include pregnant women, senior citizens, and persons with deficient immune systems.

Equipment

DOGU

■

It is perfectly possible to cook Japanese food without investing in any special equipment. The one essential is a really good knife, or, better still, a series of different knives for different purposes. However, as your interest in Japanese cookery grows, you may want to investigate some of the special pieces of equipment that the Japanese have developed.

Many items are works of sheer craftsmanship and a joy to own and use. Japanese kitchens are surprisingly low-tech and lack the labor-saving devices that we are used to, like food processors or electric mixers. Instead cooks in Japan tend to do everything by hand, using the same types of tools that have been used for generations. Japanese knives, for example, are descended from the samurai sword, and the best are collectors' items. There are also many utensils that are tailored for specific tasks and extremely handy.

You can buy basic Japanese utensils in Japanese grocery stores and some Asian import stores. Saucepans and knives, of course, can be expensive, but many of the other utensils are inexpensive, homely items that will soon come to seem indispensable.

BAMBOO ROLLING MAT *Sudare* This is a simple and very useful little contraption, a mat made of bamboo slats, rather like a bamboo placemat, which is used to roll and shape sushi, omelets, and vegetables.

CASSEROLES *Donabe* For cooking at table, the Japanese use a large and rather attractive earthenware pot that is glazed inside and unglazed outside. As tabletop cookery is very popular, these are easy to find in Japanese food and equipment shops. The alternative is to use an attractive cast-iron saucepan or any other container that can be used on top of the stove; most ordinary ceramic and ovenproof dishes cannot.

CHOPSTICKS *Hashi* In a Japanese kitchen, practically everything is done with chopsticks. Long, cooking chopsticks are used for deep-frying, stirring, mixing, and whisking, and for putting the finishing touches to a beautiful arrangement of food. There are also metal chopsticks for sashimi and an assortment of chopsticks for eating with.

DROP LID *Otoshi buta* A drop lid is made of wood (cypress or cedar) and is small enough to fit snugly inside the pot, so that it sits directly on the cooking food. It is a particularly efficient way of ensuring even cooking and of holding food in place while it cooks.

ELECTRIC RICE COOKER A rice cooker is a staple item in most Japanese kitchens. It is by far the simplest way of ensuring perfect rice all day long. You put in a measure of rice, top up the water to a set level, plug it in, and leave it. The cooker turns itself off when the rice is ready and keeps it warm for several hours. Rice cookers are sold in Chinese and Japanese shops but are, sadly, not cheap. But if you eat rice frequently a rice cooker may be a good investment.

GRATER *Oroshigane* Once discovered, you will wonder how you ever did without this! A Japanese grater is much finer than a Western one and has no holes—ideal, in fact, for grating nutmeg, as well as daikon and ginger. Most are made of metal and have a draining sill at the bottom to collect juice such as ginger juice.

KNIVES *Hocho* Japanese knives are worthy of a chapter in their own right. Designed on the same principles as the samurai sword, they have the dual qualities of strength and flexibility. The best, used by professional chefs, are made of finely honed hard carbon steel. Knives for everyday use have an inner core of hard steel forming the blade, with an outer layer of soft steel. The cheapest are stainless steel.

As with French knives, there are different shaped knives for different tasks. Sashimi knives (*sashimi bocho*) are long and thin, while vegetable knives (*nakiri bocho*) have a square blade, like a cleaver. The most useful of all is the general-purpose kitchen knife (*deba bocho*), which, like all Japanese knives, is larger than we normally use in the Western kitchen.

MORTAR AND PESTLE See *Suribachi*

RECTANGULAR FRYING PAN *Tamago-yaki nabe* In Japan, omelets are rectangular and neatly rolled—hence the existence of large and small rectangular frying pans, specially designed for making them. In the absence of one of these, use a small round omelet pan and trim the edges of the omelet.

RICE PADDLE *Shamoji* Made of smooth varnished wood or bamboo, a rice paddle is midway between a wooden spoon and a spatula. It is used for mixing and serving rice.

SKEWERS *Kushi* Grilling, often over charcoal like a barbecue, plays an essential part in Japanese cuisine and as a result every kitchen has a supply of skewers. There are long and short metal skewers (*kana gushi*) for grilling whole and sliced fish, bamboo skewers (*take gushi*) for yakitori (grilled chicken kebabs), and forked skewers for grilling tofu. Packets of bamboo skewers, like long cocktail sticks, can be bought very cheaply in Japanese and Chinese grocery stores.

STEAMER *Mushiki* The Japanese use two kinds of steamers: stacking bamboo ones, such as you see in Chinese restaurants, and large metal ones. If you don't have a steamer, it is worth investing in some bamboo ones; they are cheap, attractive, and also provide effective insulation so that food cooks more quickly. To improvise a steamer, see page 97.

SUKIYAKI PAN *Sukiyaki nabe* For an authentic sukiyaki evening, you will need a sukiyaki pan (though sukiyaki tastes equally good cooked in a heavy frying pan). A sukiyaki pan is made of cast iron and is a very attractive item, flat with shallow sides and two little handles. Like all cast-iron pans, it needs to be carefully cared for. Wash immediately after use and dry over high heat, then wipe it with oil while it is still warm. Never use detergent or dishwashing liquid.

SURIBACHI AND SURIKOGI (MORTAR AND PESTLE) Every kitchen could benefit from a Japanese mortar and pestle. In Japan, the *suribachi* is in daily use, for grinding everything from nuts and seeds to tofu and vegetables. It is such an attractive item that it is often used for serving, particularly salads. The *suribachi* is the mortar, a ceramic bowl with a heavily scored inner surface, ideal for grinding; the large wooden pestle is called a *surikogi*.

Tableware

◼

A much-quoted piece of Japanese doggerel goes something like this: "Western food—every blasted plate is round!" Plates and bowls in Japan are of every imaginable shape—round, square, rectangular, half-moon shaped, even maple leaf-shaped. They can be made of porcelain, pottery, lacquerware, or wood; sometimes even a natural leaf (such as a maple leaf or a large colorful *hoba* leaf) is used as a plate. In fact, the use of a Western-style dinner service would be taken to show a great lack of imagination! At first glance, the main criterion in arranging a place setting seems to be to ensure that no dish matches any other (though every place setting is always the same). But actually many dishes have very specific uses.

Dishes for grilled foods (*yakimono zara*) tend to be flat, rectangular, and large enough to hold a whole grilled fish; they are often rather beautiful pieces of rough sculpted earthenware. Dishes for simmered foods (*nimono zara*) are large, lidded, and made of porcelain, while rice bowls (*chawan*) are just the right size to fit in the hand. Rice bowls, too, often come with lids. Salad dishes are usually small, perhaps square-sided or round, while deep-fried foods are often served in a beautiful wicker basket. Soup bowls (*shiru-wan*) are of lacquered wood, with a domed lid. *Chawan mushi* (savory steamed custard) is served in slender porcelain cups with no handle and a flat lid, which have no other purpose. But the host usually reserves his most spectacular dishes for sashimi—large curving slabs of pottery, elegant pieces of porcelain, or lacquered wooden trays.

A table setting would not be complete without chopsticks. Japanese chopsticks are smaller than Chinese, and usually pointed at the end. They can be made of wood, lacquered wood, bamboo, or sometimes even plastic.

For guests there are special disposable chopsticks, which are used once only and then discarded. To show that they are perfectly pure and have never been used before, they are still joined together as a single piece of wood. The guest has to pull them apart to use them. Nowadays environmentally minded Japanese frown on disposable chopsticks, but many still consider it rude to give used chopsticks to a guest. However, at the newly completed Tokyo City Hall there will be plastic chopsticks, not disposable ones.

Chopsticks are always set on a chopstick rest, like a small pillow on which the tips of the chopsticks rest.

Japanese teapots tend to be small; some hold no more than two cups. They often have beautiful bamboo handles. Teacups for tea can be small and delicate or, in sushi shops, as big as a mug; but they never have handles. For sake there are flasks, which come in all sorts of shapes, and sake cups, the size of an egg cup.

SOUPS

Shirumono

Soups are an essential part of the visual feast that is Japanese cooking. There are two main types, clear soups, which are served at the beginning of a meal, and thick soups, usually made with miso, served at the end.

Soup is always served hot, in a beautiful red or black lacquered wood bowl covered with a lid. The procedure is to pick out and eat the solid ingredients with chopsticks, then drink the soup direct from the bowl. Usually you make a little slurping sound as you drink, partly to cool the soup and partly to express appreciation. As the soup cools, the lid tends to stick to the bowl; squeeze the bowl gently to release the vacuum and the lid will lift off.

Clear Soup

a flower arrangement in a bowl

SUIMONO

■

The first course to appear in a grand banquet is clear soup, a miniature flower arrangement floating in a delicate translucent broth. In fact, a clear soup is actually constructed like a flower arrangement, with three "elements," three solid ingredients that are carefully arranged in the bowl before the dashi is poured over. First comes the main ingredient, the "host"—lightly parboiled fish, seafood, or chicken, or a simmered vegetable, chosen to reflect the season. The second, the "guest," complements the first—slices of mushroom to go with shellfish, for example. The third adds a little piquancy of color and flavor—a bright sliver of lemon, shreds of fresh ginger, or a tiny leaf.

For Japanese gourmets, the soup and the sashimi are the real test of a great chef. The basis of the soup is dashi, which will flavor all the dishes to come—and if the dashi is good, you know you are in the hands of a master.

Clear Soup with Carrot and
Daikon Flowers

■

ILLUSTRATED ON PAGE 73

This is a classic and beautiful clear soup, in which the elements—noodles, red and white "flowers" and a touch of brilliant green cress—complement each other in color, texture, and taste.

Garden cress is sold at specialty produce shops from fall through spring, often in combination with mustard—ideal for this recipe. Look for the tender young shoots, about 1-inch long. If you can't find this, the top sprigs of watercress will do.

SERVES 4

4 ounces egg somen noodles	*3-4 tablespoons light soy sauce*
1 medium carrot, peeled	*1½ tablespoons sake*
2-inch slice daikon radish, peeled	*1½ tablespoons mirin*
1 bunch garden cress or watercress	*¼ teaspoon salt*
5 cups Dashi I (see pages 22-3)	

PREPARATION *Noodles:* Separate the noodles into 4 bunches and tie each bunch securely at the base with thread. To cook, bring plenty of water to a rolling boil in a large saucepan. Add the noodles, bring the water back to the boil, then top it up with ½ cup of cold water. Repeat this procedure 2 or 3 times until the noodles are *al dente*. Rinse them in cold water, drain and set aside.

To make carrot and daikon flowers: Cut the carrot into an even 3-inch cylinder. Make 5 symmetrical V-shaped cuts all the way down the cylinder and round them off to make a petal shape. Then cut off ½-inch slices of carrot to make flowers (see illustration). If you like, you can pare away part of each petal to make a more realistic flower. Repeat with the daikon to make 4 daikon flowers. Then simmer the carrot and daikon flowers in water or dashi until tender; drain.

1 Carrot flowers:
cut an even cylinder
and then make 5
lengthways slits.

2 Cut slices to
make flowers.

Cress: Separate cress into bunches of 4 or 5 stalks each; if using watercress, cut off the long, tough stems. Blanch them in rapidly boiling water for a few seconds until wilted, then drain and set aside.

TO COOK Bring the dashi just to the boil. Turn the heat to low and season with soy sauce, sake, mirin, and salt. Taste and adjust the seasoning if required.

TO SERVE Warm 4 soup bowls, then arrange a bunch of noodles, a carrot flower, a daikon flower, and a bunch of cress in each. Carefully ladle in enough hot dashi to fill the bowls ¾ full and serve immediately.

Clear Soup with Yuba

YUBA NO SUIMONO

∎

ILLUSTRATED ON PAGE 152

Yuba is bean-curd skin, the delicate creamy skin that forms on soya milk when it's simmered. The dried variety can be bought in Japanese grocery stores. It looks like sheets or ribbons of yellow parchment and can be added straight to soups without soaking. As an alternative, you could use Chinese dried bean-curd skin, which should be cut into small squares with scissors and soaked for half an hour before using.

SERVES 4

8 sprigs watercress or 8 small leaves spinach, washed and trimmed

8-12 small pieces dried yuba

1 lemon

5 cups Dashi I (see pages 22-3)

3-4 tablespoons light soy sauce

1½ tablespoons sake

1½ tablespoons mirin

¼ teaspoon salt

PREPARATION Blanch the watercress or spinach in boiling water for just 30 seconds or until wilted; rinse immediately in cold water to retain the bright green color. Break the *yuba* into small pieces, each about 1 inch square.

Lemon twists: Pare off 4 thin, neat rectangles of lemon zest each about 1 × ½ inches, taking care not to cut into the white pith. Make 2 cuts as illustrated and twist to form a triangle, crossing the ends to secure.

TO COOK Bring the dashi just to the boil. Turn the heat to low and season with soy sauce, sake, mirin, and salt. Taste and adjust the seasoning if required.

TO SERVE Arrange the *yuba* and watercress or spinach in 4 warmed soup bowls. Ladle over the hot dashi, float a lemon twist on each bowl and serve immediately.

1 Lemon twists: pare a thin rectangle of zest and make 2 slits.

2 Twist to form a triangle, crossing the ends to secure.

Clear Soup with Chicken and Egg

KAKITAMA-JIRU

■

This Japanese version of egg-drop soup includes chicken and orange carrot "flowers." It is a wonderfully rich and satisfying soup that is very easy to make. The secret of the lacy egg strands is to pour the egg very slowly onto the hot stock so that it floats on the surface.

SERVES 4

3 ounces boned and skinned chicken thigh

salt

5 teaspoons sake

1 small carrot, peeled

2 eggs (see page 31)

5 cups Dashi II (see page 22)

3 tablespoons light soy sauce

1½ tablespoons mirin

PREPARATION Dice the chicken and season with salt and 1 teaspoon sake. Cut the carrot into flowers (see page 39) or simply slice it. Simmer in dashi or water until just cooked; drain. Beat the eggs lightly; they should not become frothy.

TO COOK Bring the dashi to the boil and season with the soy sauce, the remaining sake, the mirin, and about ¼ teaspoon salt. Add the diced chicken. Reduce the heat and simmer for 2 minutes, then taste and adjust the seasoning if required.

Give the simmering dashi a stir, then pour on the eggs in a thin stream to float on the surface of the soup, stirring gently as you pour. As soon as the eggs set, turn off the heat.

TO SERVE Warm 4 soup bowls. Place 2 carrot flowers in each and ladle over the hot soup, distributing the chicken and egg evenly. Serve immediately.

Clear Soup with Prawns

EBI SUIMONO

ILLUSTRATED ON PAGE 73

In this clear soup, king prawns are transformed into flowers and complemented with dark-green spinach and a twist of brilliant-yellow lemon peel. The best prawns for this recipe are large, fresh, uncooked ones. Kuzu makes a wonderfully translucent coating for them; if it is unavailable, use cornstarch instead.

SERVES 4

4 large uncooked prawns in shell	*5 cups Dashi II (see page 23)*
¼ cup kuzu or cornstarch	*3-4 tablespoons light soy sauce*
salt	*1½ tablespoons sake*
2 ounces spinach, washed and trimmed	*1½ tablespoons mirin*
1 lemon	

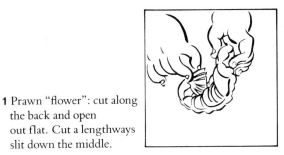

1 Prawn "flower": cut along the back and open out flat. Cut a lengthways slit down the middle.

2 Push the tail through the slit.

PREPARATION *Prawns:* Shell the prawns: twist off the head and peel off the shell and tiny legs, leaving the tail intact. Pull out the vein with a skewer, then rinse the prawns and pat them dry. Cut along the back of each and open it out flat. Then cut a lengthways slit down the middle and push the tail through to make a "flower" as illustrated above.

Grind the kuzu in a *suribachi* or mortar and pestle. Sprinkle the prawn flowers with salt and coat them lightly with kuzu. Parboil in lightly salted boiling water for 1-2 minutes until pink, then remove and drain.

Spinach: Blanch the spinach in boiling water for 30 seconds or until wilted, then rinse it immediately in cold water to retain the bright-green color. Lay the leaves evenly on a bamboo rolling mat and roll firmly to make a neat roll, squeezing out the moisture. Unroll mat, remove the spinach roll, and cut into four 2-inch cylinders.

Lemon twists: Make 4 lemon twists (see page 41).

TO COOK AND SERVE Warm 4 soup bowls and arrange a prawn and a slice of spinach in each. Bring the dashi just to the boil. Turn the heat to low and season with soy sauce, sake, mirin, and ¼ teaspoon salt; taste and adjust the seasoning if necessary. Gently ladle the dashi over the ingredients in each bowl, taking care not to disturb the arrangement. Float a lemon twist on each and serve immediately.

Thick Soup

SHIRUMONO

◼

Despite the advent of coffee and toast, a surprising number of Japanese still start the day with a bowl of thick miso soup. Miso soup marks the end of the succession of courses that makes up a banquet. And the basic home cooked meal is "a soup plus three": miso soup plus three dishes, usually sashimi, a grilled dish, and a simmered dish, followed by rice and pickles.

Miso is a wonderful Japanese invention. In the old days everyone's grandmother always made her own and stored it in the cellar under the kitchen floor. In the countryside people still do this, and one of the best souvenirs one can bring back from an out-of-town trip is a sample of the local miso.

The many varieties of miso available basically divide into two types: white miso, which is lighter, sweeter, and more suitable for summer soups, and red miso, thicker and saltier and more popular in winter soups. To make miso soup, the miso is creamed in a little hot stock and added to the soup just before serving it. Never boil miso, as this changes the taste and destroys the living enzymes.

Misos vary enormously—some are very salty, some much sweeter. Until you get to know a particular miso, always add less than the given quantity to your soup, then taste and add the rest little by little, tasting as you go, until you get the flavor that you like.

Besides miso soups, Japanese cuisine also includes a variety of thick soups, so full of meat or fish and vegetables that they are almost stews.

Classic Miso Soup

MISO SHIRU

■

ILLUSTRATED ON PAGE 152

There are as many miso soups as there are days in the year and whole cookbooks are devoted to them. The basic miso soup with which many Japanese start the day is a delicious and nutritious combination of tofu, leeks, and wakame in a rich miso-thickened broth. The smell of miso cooking first thing in the morning is always irresistible.

SERVES 4

1 small leek, washed and trimmed

5 cups Dashi II (see page 23)

a few strands dried wakame seaweed

4 ounces fresh tofu

2 tablespoons red miso

PREPARATION AND COOKING Slice the leek very finely. Bring the dashi to a simmer, add the slices of leek and simmer for 2-3 minutes until just cooked. Break the wakame seaweed into small pieces (trim off the tough stem if necessary); cut the tofu into ½-inch cubes. Add them both to the soup.

Dissolve the miso in a few tablespoons of the hot stock, blending it with a wire whisk. Stir half the mixture into the soup, then taste and add sufficient of the rest to make a rich well-flavored soup. Heat until nearly boiling.

TO SERVE Ladle the soup into 4 warmed soup bowls, distributing the leek slices, wakame, and tofu evenly, and serve immediately.

Satsuma-style Miso Soup with Vegetables

SATSUMA-JIRU

Satsuma is the area around the city of Kagoshima, on the southernmost tip of Kyushu, the southernmost of Japan's four main islands. Being nearly as far from Tokyo as it's possible to get, it has fathered some of Japan's most idiosyncratic heroes. It is also the home of a very distinctive cuisine. *Satsuma-jiru* is a rich miso soup, almost a stew, full of vegetables, including the Japanese sweet potato, the *satsuma-imo,* a native of Satsuma. If you can find it, *satsuma-age,* small cubes of deep-fried fish cake, makes a delicious addition.

SERVES 4

4 dried shiitake mushrooms, soaked in water until soft

½ medium daikon radish, peeled

1 medium carrot, peeled

1 sweet potato (satsuma-imo*), scrubbed*

4 cakes deep-fried fish cake (satsuma-age*) (optional)*

1 cake konnyaku

4½ cups Dashi II (see page 23)

3 tablespoons white miso

salt

1 green onion, very finely sliced

seven spice pepper (optional)

PREPARATION *Mushrooms:* Drain the mushrooms; cut off and discard the stalks and cut the caps into quarters.

Vegetables and fish cake: Cut the daikon and carrot into bite-sized pieces. Cut the sweet potato and fish cake into thick slices.

Konnyaku: Cut the konnyaku into chunks. To parboil it, drop it into boiling water; bring the water back to the boil, then drain and set the *konnyaku* aside.

TO COOK Put the mushroom caps into the dashi, bring it to the boil and simmer for 10 minutes. Add the carrot, daikon, and sweet potato and simmer for another few minutes. Next add the konnyaku and lastly, after another few minutes, the fish cake.

Cream the miso in a little of the dashi. Stir half the mixture into the soup, then taste and add sufficient of the rest to make a rich well-flavored soup. Heat until nearly boiling. Add a little salt if required.

TO SERVE Warm 4 soup bowls and ladle in the soup, distributing the ingredients evenly. Sprinkle a little green onion and seven spice pepper (if using) on each bowl and serve immediately.

Miso Soup with Pork

BUTANIKU MISO-SHIRU

■

A wholesome miso soup full of pork with the tang of ginger.

SERVES 4

4 ounces boneless lean pork,
   thinly sliced

2 young leeks, washed and trimmed

5 cups Dashi II (see page 23)

2-3 tablespoons red miso

2 teaspoons fresh ginger juice
   (see page 24)

PREPARATION AND COOKING Cut the pork slices across into neat ½-inch strips and the leeks into ½-inch chunks. Bring the dashi to the boil over medium high heat. Add the pork and leeks and simmer for 2 minutes. Dissolve the miso in a few tablespoons of the hot stock, blending it with a wire whisk. Stir half the mixture into the soup, then taste and add sufficient of the rest to make a rich well-flavored soup. Heat until nearly boiling.

TO SERVE Ladle the soup into 4 warmed soup bowls. Stir ½ teaspoon ginger juice into each bowl and serve immediately.

New Year's Soup

OZONI

■

For four days every year—from January 1st to January 4th—everything in Japan closes down. Tokyo is practically a ghost town as everyone goes back to their family homes in the countryside. On New Year's morning, after the traditional toast with sake, the first meal of the year is *ozoni* (literally "simmered miscellany"), a rich filling soup of vegetables, fish, and chicken with a soft sticky rice cake at the bottom. Rice cakes are regular fare at all festive occasions and always appear in *ozoni*. Apart from that, the ingredients vary region by region. In the Kansai, western Japan, *ozoni* usually includes white miso and light soy sauce. The recipe below, with chicken and vegetables, is from the Tokyo area.

Much of the preparation can be done beforehand, leaving the final assembly for the last minute.

SERVES 4

4 ounces boned and skinned chicken breast	*1 medium carrot, peeled*
1½ teaspoons light soy sauce	*4 ounces spinach, washed and trimmed*
1 teaspoon sake	*4 rice cakes (optional)*
salt	*4½ cups Dashi I or II (see pages 22-23)*
4 medium uncooked prawns	*12 slivers lemon zest*
2-inch chunk of daikon radish, peeled	

PREPARATION *Chicken:* Cut the chicken into bite-sized pieces and sprinkle lightly with 1 teaspoon soy sauce and the sake. Set aside to marinate for 15 minutes. Blanch in lightly salted water, then drain, discarding the water.

Prawns: Shell and devein the prawns, keeping the tails intact. Boil them in lightly salted water for about 2 minutes, until just pink and firm.

Daikon: Pare the daikon into a hexagonal shape, then cut it into ½-inch slices. (Hexagons are like the shell of a tortoise and the tortoise is the symbol of long life.) Simmer the daikon slices in lightly salted water for 10 minutes until they are tender; drain.

Carrot: Cut the carrot into thick slices and simmer it until it is soft; drain.

Spinach: Blanch the spinach in boiling water for 1 minute. Rinse under cold water, drain, then roll it in a bamboo mat and cut it into 1-inch lengths.

TO COOK Grill the rice cakes, if using, under a preheated hot grill for 2-3 minutes on each side so that they soften and swell; cut into quarters.

Bring the dashi to a light boil and season with ½ teaspoon salt and the remaining soy sauce. Add the chicken and simmer for 2 minutes, until it is just cooked and still very tender.

TO SERVE Warm 4 deep soup bowls and put 4 rice cake quarters in each bowl. Distribute the cooked prawns and vegetables among the bowls, then ladle over the hot dashi and chicken, dividing the chicken evenly. Float a few slivers of lemon zest on each bowl and serve immediately.

SASHIMI

Sashimi is very far from just "raw fish." It is the heart and soul of Japanese cuisine, the *pièce de résistance* of every Japanese meal. At a restaurant or a formal dinner, it is the course where the chef is let loose to give a display of pyrotechnics with his magic knife. Fish is the raw material with which he creates a landscape of food, like a miniature Japanese garden but richer and more sensual. There are slices of tuna, sinfully rich and red; the fatty belly of tuna, shaped curvaceously into roses; teetering pinnacles of white daikon radish; and sometimes a whole fish, the flesh removed and cut into slabs.

At home, sashimi is less dramatic, but the same criteria still apply. The fish must be the finest and freshest possible—so fresh that it is almost as if it has leapt from the water onto your plate. And it must be presented so that it looks as beautiful and delicate as it tastes.

As a country of islands, Japan has some of the finest fish and seafood in the world. The variety available in even the most out-of-the-way shops and markets is quite dazzling. Well before dawn every morning, lorries converge on Tokyo from all over the country, bringing fish from the coast to the great central market, Tsukiji. At five o'clock the tuna auctions begin, and early risers can watch the fishmongers competing for the best and freshest parts of the huge red fish.

One of Japan's most famous delicacies—for which there is no recipe here—is *fugu* (blowfish). Between November and March, when *fugu* is in season, restaurants hang a dried *fugu* outside, a large bloated fish, usually adorned with lipstick and a top hat. *Fugu* is one of Japan's most expensive and sought-after delicacies, not because of the taste (which is so subtle it could almost be called nondescript), but because eating it is a little like playing Russian roulette. The liver is deadly poisonous and *fugu* chefs all have to be highly trained and licensed, for a slip of the knife will contaminate the whole fish. Gourmets request the delicate flesh from right beside the liver and say that the hint of poison makes your lips tingle. And every year there are a few keen fishermen who decide to catch and clean their own, with tragic results. There is even a proverb for when you can't make your mind up: "I would like to eat *fugu;* but life too is sweet."

Any fish or seafood is delicious served as sashimi. The basic condition is that it must be the freshest possible—which means that it must be in season. The best way to ensure a supply of fresh fish is to find a reliable fishmonger—and remember, if you are to eat it raw, yesterday's fish will *not* do: it must be fresh that morning. To be absolutely sure, check for freshness yourself: check the eyes (are they clear?), the gills (are they red?), the scales (are they intact and shiny?), and the flesh (is it firm and resilient?). A fresh fish looks as if it is still alive. It has absolutely no smell. The belly is hard and elastic and the fish is firm, not floppy.

Most home cooks in Japan leave the filleting and cutting of sashimi to professionals and buy it already cut and beautifully arranged. Actually it is not difficult to cut it yourself, but you can ask your fishmonger to clean and fillet it for you. For small fish, whole fillets are best. For larger fish, like tuna, make sure that the fishmonger does not sell you a steak. You need a long rectangular piece of fillet, cut lengthways along the fish, not a steak, which is cut across the grain.

Leave your fish fillet in the refrigerator until minutes before you plan to serve it. Then skin it and cut it in one of the following ways. Be careful to handle it as little as possible; even the warmth of your hands can spoil the freshness.

If you are lucky enough to live near a Japanese grocery, buy your fish there, ready skinned and shaped, needing only to be sliced.

Skinning and Shaping Fish Fillets

■

Skinning the fillet: Lay the fillet skin-side down on a damp cutting board with the tail nearest you. Starting from the tail, hold the skin down and slide a sharp long-bladed knife between the skin and the flesh, as close to the skin as possible, so that the flesh lifts off. Keep the blade at an angle of 45 degrees. If your fingers slip on the skin, dip them into a little salt.

Shaping the fillet: Trim the fillet into an even rectangle.

Slicing Fish for Sashimi

▧

You will need a very sharp knife for cutting sashimi.

1 Thick-cut sashimi

THICK CUT *Hira Giri* Put the skinned fillet skinned-side up on a board and cut straight downwards, with the grain, firmly and neatly into domino-like slices. This is the most popular cut and is good for any fish. Red-fleshed fish like tuna are usually cut in ½-inch slices, while squid and white-fleshed fish like sea bass and sole are cut thinner, into ¼-inch slices.

2 Thin-cut sashimi

THIN CUT *Usu Zukuri* Put the skinned fillet skinned-side up on a board and cut off translucent wafer-thin slices across the grain, with the edge of the knife almost horizontal. As you cut the slices, lay them on a large plate in a circle, slightly overlapping, to make a rose. This is good for firm white-fleshed fish.

3 Cube-cut sashimi

CUBE CUT *Kaku Giri* This is most commonly used for tuna. First cut the fillet into ½-inch slices, using the thick-cut technique (see page 53), then cut the slices into ½-inch cubes.

4 Thread-cut sashimi

THREAD CUT *Ito Zukuri* This is good for squid. Cut it into ¼-inch slices, then cut the slices into long, thin ¼-inch strips and mound the strips on top of each other.

Sashimi

■

ILLUSTRATED ON PAGE 74

Sashimi is so delicious that it can be served very simply, with little more than a knob of wasabi and soy sauce to go with it. The complexity of the dish lies in the arrangement rather than in any extra flavoring. You can serve one or several varieties of fish. If you serve several, choose fish of different colors and textures—a red fish like salmon or tuna, a white fish like bass, and squid, for example.

Shiso (perilla or beefsteak plant) is a relative of mint with large green leaves and a delightfully refreshing tang. It makes a perfect foil for sashimi. Easy to grow (in Japan it grows like a weed) *shiso* is sold at Japanese grocery stores; if you can't find it, you could replace it with something green and refreshing like parsley.

SERVES 4

thread-cut daikon radish (see page 56)

3-4 shiso leaves, or sprigs parsley, washed and patted dry

1 tablespoon wasabi powder

soy sauce or dipping sauce (see pages 59-61)

1 pound very fresh raw fish (salmon, trout, tuna, sea bass, sea bream (Tai snapper), flounder, mackerel, squid, etc.)

PREPARATION Prepare the daikon and *shiso* leaves. Mix the wasabi with water to make a thick, dryish paste. Lay out small bowls for soy sauce or the dipping sauce. Lastly, slice the fish, following the cutting techniques described above.

TO SERVE Choose a beautiful serving dish and make piles of daikon threads on it. Arrange several slices of fish together, like dominoes, leaning on the piles, and use the *shiso* or parsley to garnish. Make the wasabi into a small mound and put it on the dish. Serve immediately, with sauce to dip.

Decorative Garnishes

You will need a very sharp knife for these—and most are easier said than done! Besides the following garnishes, you can also use thinly sliced lemon, parsley, *shiso* leaves, shredded carrot or cucumber, wakame seaweed, and leaves and flowers such as small chrysanthemums.

TO MAKE A "ROSE" Cut tapering slices of salmon, tuna, or squid. Lay them end to end, slightly overlapping, then roll up carefully to form a rose. You can also layer slices of flounder with slices of lemon, beginning and ending with a slice of lemon. Or make rolls of flounder slices, stand them upright, and top with a few salmon roe.

1 Thread-cut daikon: peel into a long continuous sheet.

2 Cut into 8-inch lengths, stack, then cut into fine threads.

THREAD-CUT DAIKON RADISH Sashimi is always served on a bed of daikon, cut into fine threads. Carrots can be cut in the same way and, if daikon is not available, make a good alternative.

Take a daikon and cut a 4-inch length. Peel it. Then, holding it in one hand, pare it with the other into a long continuous even sheet, transparently thin, using your thumb to control and steady the knife (see illustration). Cut into 8-inch lengths, stack the sheets and cut them across into fine threads. Set them aside in a bowl of cold water to soften. Just before using, drain and pat dry on paper toweling. The faint-hearted can buy ready-cut daikon threads in Japanese grocery stores—or simply shred daikon on a grater.

1 Cucumber pine leaves: score the skin very closely with deep cuts.

2 Cut and push the skin with your thumb first one way then the other.

CUCUMBER PINE LEAVES *Matsuba* This is a very spectacular garnish, reminiscent of the leaves or needles spraying out on a Japanese pine tree.

Use the straightest cucumber you can find. First soften the skin to make it pliable and elastic: dampen it, rub well with salt, and leave it for a few minutes. Then boil the cucumber for 1-2 minutes. Drain and immerse it in cold running water.

Cut off a 4-inch length and slice it in half lengthways. Lay one half cut-side down on a cutting board and quickly score the skin fairly deeply in a series of lengthways cuts, as close together as possible.

Now comes the difficult part! Starting at the bottom of the cucumber, with the knife tip away from you, make a shallow horizontal cut down into the cucumber, pushing the strip of skin across the blade *at the same time*. The cut skin will feather out like the needle sprays of a pine tree. Carry on cutting and pushing, first one way, then the other, all the way up the cucumber (see illustration). The trick is to do all this very quickly, while the skin is still soft.

1 Mountain peaks: cut through the center, then make a diagonal cut as far as the central incision.

2 Repeat on the other side and separate.

MOUNTAIN PEAKS *Yamagata* Cucumbers and carrots can be turned into decorative mountain peaks. Peel carrots but leave cucumbers with their green skin. Cut a 1½-inch length of carrot or cucumber. First make a vertical cut through the center, halfway down, leaving the ends intact. Then lay the carrot or cucumber on its side, with the cut horizontal, and make a diagonal cut from top left to mid right, as far as the central incision. Roll over 180 degrees and repeat exactly—i.e. make another cut, also from top left to mid right. This is actually not as complicated as it sounds. The 2 cut pieces come apart to make "mountain peaks."

Seasonings

▪

The seasoning *par excellence* for sashimi is wasabi, the stingingly hot, green substance that brings tears to the eyes. It can be found in its dried form, to be mixed with water like mustard, or in a tube. In Japan, the best sashimi is invariably served with fresh wasabi, freshly grated. Other seasonings include freshly grated ginger root and paper-thin shreds of green onion, rinsed in cold water and drained.

RED MAPLE RADISH *Momiji Oroshi* A spicy variation on grated daikon, chilies give a fiery tang and a red coloring to it.

Cut a 2-inch piece of daikon radish, peel it and make 3 or 4 holes in one end with a chopstick. Deseed 3 or 4 dried chilies and push them into the holes. If you have time, leave the daikon to rest for up to 1 hour; the chilies absorb the daikon juices and soften and flavor the daikon.

Grate the daikon (together with the chilies) on a Japanese grater or a very fine-toothed grater. Squeeze the resulting mixture in muslin or gauze to remove as much water as possible, then shape into small mounds.

Dipping Sauces

▪

The basic sauce for sashimi is soy sauce. For sashimi, it is often diluted with sake—about 1 part sake to 3 parts soy sauce. Besides this, the most popular dipping sauce is Tosa soy sauce, flavored with bonito flakes.

Tosa Soy Sauce

TOSA JOYU

■

MAKES ABOUT 1 CUP

Tosa is the old name for the southern part of Shikoku island, where the best bonito comes from.

5 teaspoons sake

2 tablespoons mirin

2-inch square dried kombu, wiped

1 cup dark soy sauce

good handful dried bonito flakes

Heat the sake and mirin in a small saucepan until it produces fumes, then light the fumes with a long-handled match to burn off the alcohol (this step can be omitted if you like). Combine all the ingredients in a bowl and leave for 24 hours, then strain the liquid into a jar, cover and store in a dark cool place for at least 1 month to mature. This sauce is best after 6 months and keeps for up to 3 years.

Here is a simpler version, which can be used immediately:

MAKES ABOUT ½ CUP

½ cup soy sauce

2 tablespoons sake

good handful dried bonito flakes

Put all the ingredients in a small saucepan and bring to the boil. Set aside to cool, then strain and use.

Soy sauce flavored with sesame seeds, wasabi, or ginger is easy to make and provides a pleasant variation of flavors.

Wasabi Soy Sauce

WASABI JOYU

■

MAKES ABOUT ½ CUP

½ tablespoon wasabi powder

1 tablespoon mirin

½ cup soy sauce

Blend the wasabi with the mirin to make a paste, then gradually mix in the soy sauce.

Ginger Soy Sauce

SHOGA JOYU

■

MAKES ABOUT ½ CUP

1 tablespoon freshly grated ginger root

1 tablespoon mirin

½ cup soy sauce

Mix the ingredients together and use immediately.

Ponzu Sauce

■

MAKES ABOUT 2½ CUPS

1 cup freshly squeezed lemon juice

½ cup rice vinegar

1 cup dark soy sauce

3 tablespoons mirin

2-inch square dried kombu, wiped

handful dried bonito flakes

Put the ingredients in a bowl and leave overnight. The following day, strain the sauce into a jar, cover, and store in the refrigerator until you are ready to use it. The sauce keeps for 3 months.

GRILLED, FRIED, AND BAKED DISHES

Yakimono

Most meals in Japan, even the simplest, include a grilled dish, often a whole fish, curved as if it was still swimming through the sea, flecked with salt like specks of foam. Grilling is surely the most ancient method of cooking. In man's hunting days, he used to cook freshly caught meat or fish over an open fire. In the West, we still barbecue in the summer and char-grilling is growing is popularity, but baking is much more common. Conversely, in Japan, oven-baking is a very recent development, but the process of grilling has been refined into a fine art.

Many of Japan's most popular eating houses still feature foods cooked over an open flame. *Robatayaki* restaurants are noisy drinking and eating establishments where the customers sit along the counter and the chefs grill meat and vegetables over charcoal and pass them across, precariously balanced on a wooden paddle. Then there are *yakitori* bars, small and smoky, the sort of place where tired businessmen escape for a few skewers of grilled chicken and some banter with the maestro on their way home from work. Eel is another charcoal-grilled dish. In eel restaurants, the customers can watch while the chefs turn the tender fillets (Japanese eel is a fraction of the size of European eel) and brush them with paint-brush-loads of a rich sweet soy-based sauce.

Like foods eaten raw, foods to be grilled must be of the finest quality. The process of grilling is quite simple, but less easy to carry out to perfection. The essence is to cook the food—fish, meat, chicken, or vegetables—quickly, over a high heat, so that the outside crisps while the inside remains tender and succu-lent. The secret is to stop cooking when the heat has barely reached the center of the food but the outside is already crisp and brown.

Many Western homes are not equipped for this type of grilling. In Japan chefs usually grill over charcoal and a special smokeless and very hot charcoal has been developed for the purpose. As the aim is heat, not smoke, a preheated hot broiler or an improvised "barbecue" over a gas burner are perfectly adequate alterna-tives. And the recently marketed stovetop grills are an ideal solution.

The category of *yakimono* also includes fried and baked foods. In many of the following dishes the main ingredient—meat or fish—can be either grilled or fried.

Grilled Dishes

skewering techniques

■

Most foods to be grilled are first skewered, with two aims: to hold the shape of the food while it cooks and to make sure it cooks efficiently, all the way through. There are a variety of different techniques, designed to make the food look as attractive as possible.

Thin metal barbecue skewers in different lengths are the most convenient to use, though bamboo skewers are traditionally called for in a few specific dishes. When using bamboo skewers, they should be soaked for at least 10 minutes before use so that they don't burn. The methods described below are illustrated on page 65.

LENGTHWAYS SKEWERING *Tate Gushi* The most common method of skewering fish is to skewer it along the grain. Steadying the fish with one hand, slide skewers lengthways into the fish, taking care not to pierce the surface.

FLAT SKEWERING *Hira Gushi* To skewer several pieces of fillet together, push the skewers in across the grain; this is a good way of making sure that the fish doesn't flake off while cooking.

SIDE SKEWERING *Yoko Gushi* To skewer several small fish together, lay them side by side and insert 3 or 4 skewers.

ONE-TUCK SKEWERING *Kata Tsuma Ore* This method of skewering is named after the Japanese habit of tucking your kimono into your belt while you work. To give thin flat fillets a little more shape and character, tuck one side of the fillet under and hold it in place with skewers.

TWO-TUCK SKEWERING *Ryo Tsuma Ore* Tucking both sides under ensures that the inside remains moist and tender during cooking.

STITCH SKEWERING *Nui Gushi* This is a method of skewering for squid. Lay the squid out flat, hold it in place with one hand, and thread skewers through like stitches to make a fan shape. One short skewer threaded through diagonally holds the whole thing in place.

Skewering Fish

1 Lengthways skewering

2 Flat skewering

3 Side skewering

4 One-tuck skewering

5 Two-tuck skewering

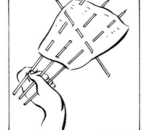

6 Stitch skewering

Salt-Grilled Whole Fish

SUGATA-YAKI

■

ILLUSTRATED ON PAGE 75

The first thing to know about a fish is that it has a "front" and a "back." Lay the fish with its head facing to the left and its belly toward you and you are looking at the front. This is the side that is uppermost when the fisherman places it in his basket, head to the left; and it is the side that should face you when you lay it on the plate, still with the head to the left. (There are some exceptions—flat fish, of course, are always laid with their top side uppermost and some may end up facing to the right.)

A whole fish simply grilled and served with a dash of lemon or a drop of soy sauce is a gourmet's delight and one of the masterpieces of Japanese cuisine. To make sure that it looks attractive on the plate, grill the back first, and then the front (if you are grilling over charcoal, this is reversed—front first, then back). Turn the fish only once: every time it is turned, precious juices drip out. Any small to medium fish can be salt-grilled. For the very best flavor you need to grill over charcoal, but of course you can salt-grill on or under any type of grill.

SERVES 4

4 rainbow trout, small mackerel, or any other small or medium-sized fish

salt

lemon wedges

soy sauce

PREPARATION *Skewering:* Clean, scale, and gut the fish, leaving the head and tail intact. Holding each fish with the head pointing to the right and the back towards you, feed 1 skewer (for a small fish) or 2 parallel skewers (for a larger one) through the back, beginning just below the eye and ending 2 inches before the tail (see illustration), so that the fish curves into an "S" with its tail standing up. The skewers should go only through the flesh of the fish, not out the other side; be careful not to puncture the front. Prick the skin a few times with a needle to prevent blistering and shrinking.

Salting: Take a generous pinch of salt and rub it into the tail and fins, so that they are heavily coated. This is "cosmetic" salting. It prevents tail and fins from burning and makes an attractive snowy crust when cooked. Then rub the entire fish with salt. If you like, wrap the tail and fins in foil to stop them from burning. Set the fish aside to rest after salting for at least 10 minutes; a large fish will need 30 minutes.

TO COOK Grill the fish over a hot flame or under a hot broiler. If you are cooking the traditional Japanese way, *over* a flame, cook the *front* of the fish first. When it is half done and pinkish bubbles form on the skin, turn it and grill the back. Rotate the skewers once or twice to stop them from sticking but be sure only to turn the fish once. Remove it from the heat when it is just done and carefully pull out the skewers. If you are cooking *under* the broiler, reverse the order: cook the *back* of the fish first, followed by the front.

TO SERVE Lay each fish on its own plate with the head facing to the left. Garnish with lemon wedges and serve piping hot with soy sauce.

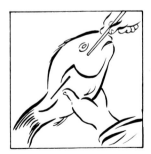

Skewering a whole fish.

Yakitori

GRILLED CHICKEN KEBABS

■

ILLUSTRATED ON PAGE 76

Some of Tokyo's best food is to be found hidden away under the railway tracks, in tiny restaurants that seat no more than four customers, with a fifth balanced on a stool propping open the door. Here a chef labors away over a smoking charcoal brazier, grilling up delicious kebabs of skewered chicken. Most chefs have their own secret recipe for the wonderful sweet sauce that coats the grilled chicken, and many use the same sauce year after year, topping it up but never changing it, letting the chicken juices drip into it to make it richer and richer.

The best part of the chicken for yakitori is the tender thigh meat; the breast is not usually used. Restaurants always serve every imaginable part of the chicken—the liver, wings, heart, gizzard, tongue, intestines, and even skin all make delicious yakitori.

Yakitori is an ideal party dish. The sauce can be made and the cutting and skewering done well in advance, leaving just the grilling for the last minute. It is also an ideal dish for a barbecue.

Equipment: You will need 15-20 eight-inch bamboo skewers that have been soaked or metal barbecue skewers.

SERVES 4

YAKITORI SAUCE

2 cups soy sauce

1 cup chicken stock

1 cup sake

1 cup mirin

½ cup sugar

7 ounces chicken livers

4 fresh shiitake or other fresh mushrooms, wiped

4 small green bell peppers, deseeded

*12 ounces boned chicken thigh,
with skin*

*3 thin young leeks, washed and
trimmed, or 3 fat green
onions*

seven spice pepper

PREPARATION *Yakitori sauce:* Combine all the ingredients in a small saucepan. Bring to the boil, reduce the heat and simmer for 10-15 minutes until the sauce is reduced by one-third. Remove from the heat and cool to room temperature, then pour the sauce into a deep screw-topped jar to store it. The yakitori sauce can be used for several meals but should be kept tightly sealed in the refrigerator.

Chicken and chicken livers: Cut the chicken and the chicken livers into 1-inch cubes. Put the livers into a bowl of cold water to soak for 5 minutes.

Vegetables: Cut off and discard the mushroom stalks; if the caps are large, cut them into halves or quarters. Cut the peppers into 1-inch chunks and the leeks into ½-inch sections. All the different ingredients should be about the same size.

Thread the ingredients onto the skewers, leaving a little space between each piece for even cooking; each skewer will hold 4 or 5 pieces. Prepare skewerfuls of chicken, chicken livers, mixed vegetables, and chicken and leeks alternately, beginning and ending with chicken.

TO COOK Grill over the hottest flame or broil under the highest heat, turning frequently to avoid burning. After a few seconds, when the juices begin to drip, baste the skewers with the yakitori sauce. Return to the heat and carry on cooking, basting with the sauce, until the chicken is lightly cooked but still moist. The total cooking time is about 5-10 minutes.

TO SERVE Serve the yakitori piping hot, on its skewers, and spoon over a little extra yakitori sauce. In Japan yakitori is usually eaten sprinkled with seven spice pepper (see page 28).

Salt-Grilled Yakitori

SHIO YAKITORI

In Japanese cooking, the simple is often the best. Many gourmets prefer their yakitori simply salt-grilled and served with a slice of lemon.

SERVES 4

*8 small chicken thighs, boned,
     with skin*

2 tablespoons sake

salt

lemon wedges

PREPARATION Sprinkle the chicken thighs with sake and leave for 5–10 minutes to tenderize. Then skewer them in pairs on 2 skewers per pair. Sprinkle both sides liberally with salt.

TO COOK Grill over a hot flame or under a hot broiler for about 10 minutes on each side, until the skin is nicely charred and the flesh cooked but still moist.

TO SERVE Serve on the skewers, garnished with lemon wedges.

Miso Yakitori

■

A simple chicken and leek yakitori, brushed with a rich miso sauce.

SERVES 4

MISO SAUCE

3 tablespoons red or white miso

2 tablespoons sugar

3 tablespoons sake

2 tablespoons mirin

12 ounces boned chicken thighs, with skin

2 thin young leeks, washed and trimmed, or 2 fat green onions

PREPARATION Soak long bamboo skewers in water for at least 10 minutes.

Miso sauce: Mix together all the ingredients in a small saucepan and heat, stirring well, until the sauce is smooth and the sugar dissolves.

Chicken and leeks: Cut the chicken into 1-inch cubes and the leeks into 1½-inch chunks. Thread the chicken and leeks alternately onto skewers, 3 pieces of chicken and 2 of leek to each skewer; finish off the chicken by making a few skewers with chicken only.

TO COOK Grill over a very hot flame or under a very hot broiler, turning occasionally, until the chicken is nearly done. Brush with the miso sauce and continue cooking, then turn and brush the other side. Repeat this process once or twice until the chicken and leeks are cooked.

TO SERVE Serve immediately on the skewers. Leftover miso sauce can be stored in the refrigerator in a covered container and used again.

Grilled Tofu with
Flavored Miso

TOFU DENGAKU

■

Everyone knows that tofu is good for you, but quite what to do with it is another matter. In Japan there is no such problem. Tofu is an everyday food, used regularly in home cooking. But it is particularly associated with temple cuisine. Grilled tofu, skewered on a two-pronged bamboo stick and topped with sweetened miso, is served in temples all over Japan. It is always dressed with several different misos—red, white, even green—which makes it good to look at as well as good for you. In fact, it is almost more of a snack than a food.

Tofu is fairly delicate and needs to be handled with care. The best sort for grilling is fresh tofu, made daily and sold in Chinese markets.

You will need 40 bamboo skewers or, better still, if you can find them, 20 two-pronged tofu skewers for this dish. Otherwise, flat "lolly sticks" or wooden forks would do. Soak them for at least 10 minutes before you start grilling to prevent them from burning.

The quantities in the recipe make quite a lot of flavored miso. Either make only one color, or store leftover miso in a covered container in the refrigerator, where it will keep for 1–2 months.

SERVES 4

1 pound fresh tofu	1 tablespoon mirin
FLAVORED WHITE MISO	1 tablespoon sugar
3 tablespoons white miso	1 egg yolk (see page 31)
1 tablespoon sake	1-2 tablespoons dashi (see page 22)

Clear soup with carrot and daikon flowers (page 38); Clear soup with prawns (page 42).

73

Mixed sashimi on a bed of thread-cut daikon, decorated with cucumber pine leaves and served with wasabi and shiso leaves: slices of raw flounder, squid, and tuna; raw prawns, "roses" of salmon, squid, and mackerel with grated egg yolk; rolls of flounder topped with salmon roe (see pages 55-8).

Salt-grilled whole trout (page 66), garnished with lemon wedges, parsley, cucumber, and daikon radish.

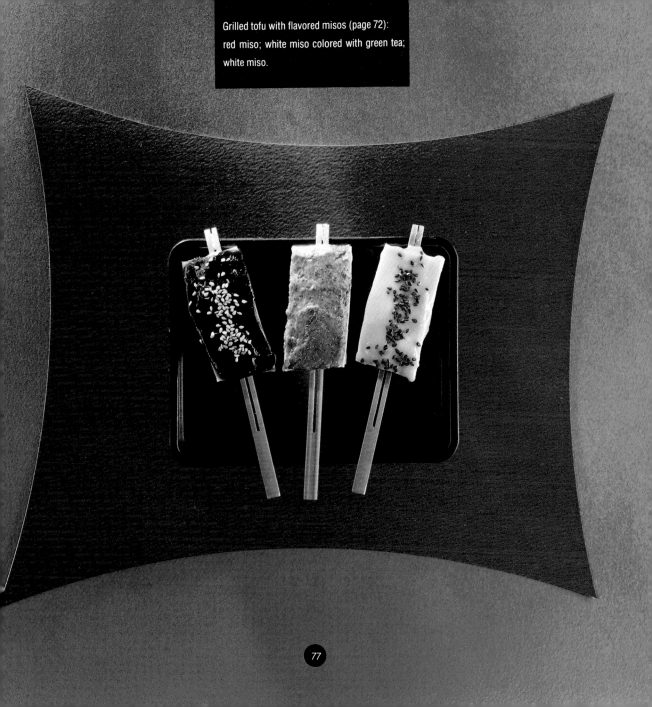

Grilled tofu with flavored misos (page 72):
red miso; white miso colored with green tea;
white miso.

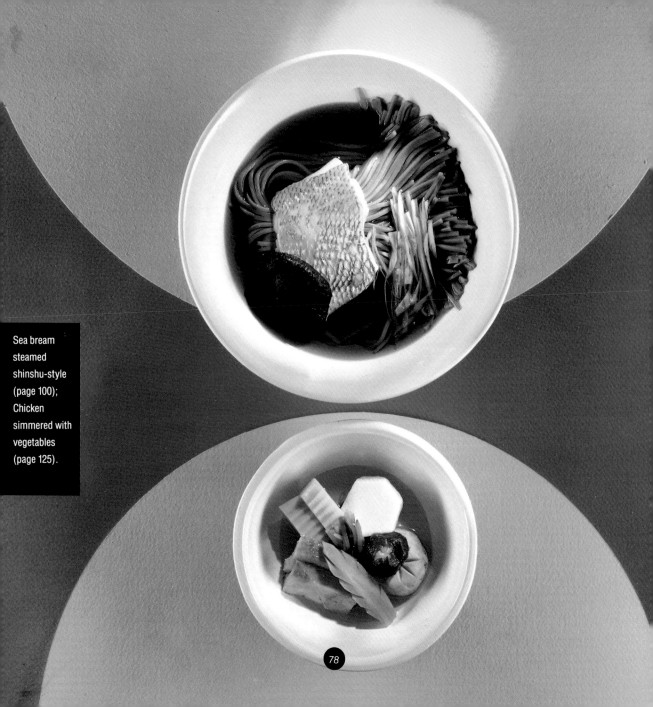

Sea bream
steamed
shinshu-style
(page 100);
Chicken
simmered with
vegetables
(page 125).

Sole simmered in sake (page 120); Savory steamed custard-in-a-cup (page 103).

Mixed tempura (page 109) and dipping sauce;
Chrysanthemum turnip (page 142).

FLAVORED RED MISO

3 tablespoons red miso

1 tablespoon sake

1 tablespoon mirin

1 tablespoon sugar

1 egg yolk (see page 31)

1-2 tablespoons dashi (see page 22)

GARNISH

white sesame seeds, lightly toasted
   (see page 28)

black sesame seeds, lightly toasted
   (see page 28)

PREPARATION *Tofu:* Cut the tofu in half and then slice to make 12 rectangular matchbox-sized pieces, each about 2½ × 1½ × ¾ inches. Lay them between tea towels to drain. The tofu should be left for at least 1 hour to drain and firm up.

Bamboo skewers or tofu skewers: Soak bamboo skewers or two-pronged tofu skewers in water for at least 10 minutes.

Flavored misos: Mix the white miso, sake, mirin, sugar, and egg yolk in the top of a double boiler, and heat over simmering water, stirring constantly, until the mixture thickens. Add enough of the dashi to give a thick creamy consistency. Remove from the heat. Prepare the red miso in the same way as the white.

TO COOK Slide 2 bamboo skewers (or 1 two-pronged tofu skewer) lengthways right through each piece of tofu and out the other end. Grill the tofu over hot charcoal or under a preheated very hot broiler for 2 minutes on each side, until the outside becomes dry and begins to speckle brown; the inside should still be soft and moist.

Spread half the tofu slices with red miso and half with white miso—use a knife to spread it right to the edges of the tofu—and return to the grill with the miso side towards the heat. Grill for 1 minute until heated through.

TO SERVE Garnish the red miso with white sesame seeds and the white miso with black sesame seeds. Alternatively, you could garnish the red miso with shreads of lemon rind and the white with a tiny fresh coriander leaf, washed and patted dry.

Serve 3 skewers to each person.

Fried Dishes

∎

Teriyaki

SWEET-GLAZED FISH OR MEAT

∎

Teriyaki is one of the most famous Japanese dishes—succulent slices of fish, beef, or chicken, glazed with a wonderfully sweet soy-based sauce, which gives a shiny gloss. As always, the very best teriyaki sauce is homemade; you can make a fairly large quantity and keep it indefinitely in the refrigerator. But to save time, there are also acceptable commercial sauces available.

Salmon Teriyaki

SAKE TERIYAKI

∎

Oily fish is best for teriyaki; the glaze tends to overwhelm the taste of more delicate fish. Salmon, mackerel, fresh tuna, and halibut all make delicious teriyaki, as do scallops, which are an alternative in this recipe. Buy fish fillets or steaks complete with skin; both thick and thin salmon steaks work well in this recipe.

SERVES 4

2 small salmon steaks

salt

4 ounces fresh mushrooms, wiped

4 small tomatoes

2 ounces bean sprouts, washed
   and trimmed

2 ounces snow peas, topped and tailed

vegetable oil

TERIYAKI SAUCE

¼ cup dark soy sauce

¼ cup sake

2 tablespoons mirin

1 tablespoon sugar

PREPARATION *Salmon:* Rinse the salmon steaks under cold water and pat dry. Cut them in half lengthways to make 4 pieces and cut out the bone. Rinse the salmon again and pat dry.

Vegetables: Cut off and discard the mushroom stalks and cut a neat cross in each cap (see page 111). Halve the tomatoes, trim the bean sprouts, and cut the snow peas diagonally into 1-inch slices.

Teriyaki sauce: Mix the ingredients in a saucepan and stir over medium heat until the sugar has dissolved. The sauce can be used immediately or cooled and refrigerated. Marinate the salmon in a little sauce for 10 minutes. Drain, reserving the marinade.

TO COOK Heat a little oil in a frying pan and sauté the vegetables for 2-3 minutes until they are cooked through but still crisp. Remove, drain, and keep warm.

Wipe out the frying pan and add a little fresh oil. Heat the oil and sauté the salmon over medium to high heat for 1-2 minutes, until slightly browned; turn gently and brown the other side. Be careful not to overcook.

Drain off excess oil so that the pan is fairly dry. Pour a little teriyaki sauce over the salmon and continue to cook for a few minutes, turning and basting the steaks so that they are well coated.

TO SERVE Remove the salmon from the pan and serve on individual plates. Simmer the remaining teriyaki sauce until it is thick and syrupy and with big bubbles; be careful not to over-reduce it, as it burns easily. Spoon the sauce over the fish, add the warm vegetables, and serve immediately.

Alternatively, grill the salmon: thread each piece on 2 skewers, brush with oil and broil under high heat for 2-3 minutes on each side. Twist the skewers from time to time to stop them from sticking.

While the salmon is grilling, simmer the sauce over medium heat until it becomes thick and syrupy, and starts to make large bubbles as it boils.

When the salmon is nearly cooked, brush with the reduced sauce a few times and continue cooking until the salmon flakes easily when tested with a fork. Serve with the sautéed vegetables.

Chicken Teriyaki

TORI TERIYAKI

■

ILLUSTRATED ON PAGE 152

Sweet teriyaki sauce makes a delicious complement for the mild taste of chicken.

SERVES 4

2 chicken thighs, boned	*vegetable oil*
8 ounces broccoli, washed and trimmed	*1 recipe Teriyaki sauce (see page 82)*
salt	*seven spice pepper*

PERPARATION *Chicken:* Prick the chicken skin all over with a fork so that the sauce can penetrate.

Broccoli: Break the broccoli into florets and cook in lightly salted boiling water for 2-3 minutes, until just tender; the stalks should still be a little crisp. Drain and set the florets aside.

TO COOK Brush a frying pan with oil and put in the chicken, skin side down. Sauté it for a few minutes until it is browned on all sides. If there is a lot of oil in the pan, tip out the excess. Pour the teriyaki sauce into the pan, bring it to the boil, and cook the chicken in the sauce for about 10 minutes, turning occasionally, until the chicken is well cooked and tender and the sauce is reduced.

Take the chicken out of the pan. The sauce should be thick and syrupy. If not, boil it for a few minutes more until it is fully reduced and boiling with big bubbles. (Beware: do not overcook the sauce as it burns easily.)

TO SERVE Cut the chicken across into ½-inch slices. Arrange them on 4 plates and spoon over the teriyaki sauce; sprinkle over a little seven spice pepper, add the broccoli, and serve immediately.

Pork Fried with Ginger

BUTANIKU SHOGA-YAKI

■

This delicious dish of pork sautéed with ginger and soy sauce is made very quickly over high heat. Ask your butcher to cut paper-thin slices of pork for you. To cut it yourself, semi-freeze it for 30–40 minutes until it is firm but not frozen; this will make it much easier to cut.

SERVES 4

1 pound pork loin, very finely sliced

2 ounces bean sprouts, washed and trimmed

vegetable oil

SAUCE

1 tablespoon dashi (see page 22)

1 tablespoon dark soy sauce

1 tablespoon sake

1 tablespoon mirin

1 teaspoon fresh ginger juice (see page 24)

PREPARATION Cut the pork slices into 2-inch pieces. Blanch the bean sprouts in boiling water; drain. Mix the sauce ingredients in a small bowl and stir until the sugar dissolves.

TO COOK Heat a little oil in a frying pan and sauté half the pork just until it changes color; repeat with the remaining half and remove it from the pan. Pour in the sauce, bring it to the boil, and simmer until it has reduced by one-third. Return the pork to the pan, add the bean sprouts and cook for 1–2 minutes, just until both are heated through. Remove from the heat.

TO SERVE Serve immediately on individual plates, spooning the sauce over the pork and bean sprouts.

Beef and Vegetable Rolls

GYUNIKU YASAI-MAKI

This is a colorful and tasty dish of beef rolled around an assortment of vegetables. It can be served hot or at room temperature
and makes a delicious party dish. Ask your butcher to cut the
beef into paper-thin slices for you on a bacon slicer (he will
need to semi-freeze it first).

SERVES 4

4 ounces carrot, peeled

4 ounces asparagus, trimmed

4 ounces green beans, topped and tailed

salt

12 ounces boneless beef sirloin,
  sliced paper thin

cornstarch

vegetable oil

4 sprigs watercress

MARINADE

¼ cup water

1 tablespoon sugar

1 tablespoon sake

1 tablespoon mirin

3 tablespoons soy sauce

PREPARATION *Vegetables:* Cut the carrot into chunks about 4 inches long, then
into thin sticks. Cut the asparagus into pieces of a similar size. Simmer the vegetables separately in lightly salted water until tender. The asparagus and beans
should be refreshed in cold water after cooking, to preserve their color. Drain
all the vegetables and pat them dry.

Beef: Lay out a slice of beef flat on a chopping board. Sift cornstarch lightly
over it to hold the vegetables in place. Take about 3 pieces of carrot, 3 sticks of
asparagus, and beans and lay them together at one end of the strip. Roll up the
beef firmly and tie the roll with string in the middle and towards the ends, or
secure it with wooden toothpicks. Continue in the same way until all the beef
and vegetables are used.

Marinade: Mix the marinade ingredients and put the rolls in to marinate for 1 hour, turning them occasionally. Drain, reserving the marinade. (You can omit the marinating if you are in a hurry.)

TO COOK Heat a little oil in a frying pan and sauté the rolls over medium heat for 1 minute or so to brown them on all sides. Pour over the marinade, bring to the boil, and simmer over low heat for 2-3 minutes, until the beef is well flavored and tender and the marinade has thickened.

TO SERVE Cut the strings with scissors and slice the rolls into quarters. Arrange several pieces on small individual plates and spoon over a little of the marinade. Garnish with watercress.

An alternative method of cooking the rolls is to skewer them—2 skewers will hold 3 or 4 rolls—and broil them under high heat, turning them so that both sides are well cooked. Once the color has changed, baste the rolls several times with the marinade. Reduce the marinade in a pan and spoon it over the rolls before serving.

Teppanyaki

MIXED GRILL

∎

Teppanyaki is the Japanese way of cooking steak. It is a new-comer to the Japanese cooking scene and only developed after the Second World War, once meat had become widely available. Customers to teppanyaki restaurants sit around a counter topped with a gleaming stainless steel plate, where the chefs take it upon themselves to provide entertainment as well as food, juggling their knives and performing miraculous cutting feats while sautéing a mouth-watering combination of steak, sea-foods, and vegetables.

At home it's a tamer affair but no less delicious. To make teppanyaki you will need an electric frying pan or griddle or a heating unit at the table with a heavy frying pan on it.

The selection and quantity of the ingredients really depends on the taste and appetite of the diners. The following is just one possible selection. All the preparation can be done several hours in advance. Refrigerate the ingredients separately and arrange them on a platter just before serving.

SERVES 4

3-ounce slice beef tenderloin

4 sea scallops

4 uncooked prawns, shelled and deveined

1 medium onion, peeled

2 baby leeks or green onions, washed and trimmed

2 ounces fresh shiitake or button mushrooms, wiped

½ green bell pepper, deseeded

2 ounces snow peas, topped and tailed

2 ounces bean sprouts, washed and trimmed

vegetable oil or beef suet

CONDIMENTS

*freshly grated daikon radish
(see page 21)*

green onions, chopped very finely

seven spice pepper

*powdered English mustard,
mixed with water*

SAUCES

Ponzu sauce (see page 61)

Sesame sauce (see page 165)

PREPARATION Trim the steaks and cut them across into ¼-inch thick slices. Wash the scallops and cut off the gristle around the central fleshy part; cut the scallops in half if they are plump. Rinse the prawns.

Vegetables: Slice the onion (before you cut each slice, insert a toothpick across the rings to keep them together and slice down beside it; see page 111). Cut the leeks into 2-inch lengths. Cut off and discard the mushroom stalks; cut a decorative cross in each mushroom cap (see page 111). Cut the pepper lengthways into eighths.

Arrange the beef, seafood, and vegetables on 1 or 2 large platters.

TO COOK AND SERVE Set an electric frying pan or a griddle in the center of the table. Serve the sauces in gravy boats or jugs and the condiments in small bowls and provide each place with a dipping bowl to mix the sauces and condiments.

Brush the frying pan with a little oil and fry the meat, seafood, and vegetables—a few pieces at a time, over medium heat—turning, until they are done. Between each batch of food, wipe off the surface of the pan with a cloth dipped in cooking oil, so that it stays clean. The diners serve themselves from the pan and dip the food into one of the sauces before eating it.

Eggplant with Flavored Miso

NASU DENGAKU

■

This is a favorite of Tokyo's little drinking houses as well as a popular dish to cook at home.

SERVES 4

2 large Japanese eggplants

vegetable oil

flavored white and red misos

black and white sesame seeds, toasted (see page 28)

PREPARATION Halve the eggplants lengthways, cutting straight through the stalks. With a sharp knife, score deeply right around the edge of the flesh and cross-score the cut face to make a crisscross pattern, or make 3 cuts straight across it; this makes the cooked eggplant easier to eat with chopsticks. You can also cut a slender slice off the base of the "boat" to make it more stable. Globular Western eggplant can be cut across into thick 1-inch slices.

Soak the eggplant in cold water to remove bitterness. Drain and lightly squeeze them, then pat dry before cooking.

TO COOK You can either fry or broil the eggplant.

To broil, thread each eggplant "boat" on bamboo skewers that have been soaked in water for at least 10 minutes. Brush both sides with oil and broil under a very hot broiler for about 5 minutes on each side, brushing with oil occasionally if required; turn the eggplant once only, and test if it is done with a toothpick. The flesh should be very soft.

To fry, brush a frying pan with oil and fry the eggplant, covered, over medium heat for about 10 minutes or until very soft, turning once. Drain well on paper toweling to remove as much oil as possible.

TO SERVE Spread flavored miso on each eggplant half, using a knife to make it even, and smoothing it right to the edges. Using both red and white miso on each eggplant "boat," with a sharp division between them, looks very attractive. Sprinkle a line of black sesame seeds on the white miso and white sesame seeds on the red. Serve hot or at room temperature.

Rolled Omelet

DASHIMAKI TAMAGO

■

ILLUSTRATED ON PAGE 76

Every Japanese kitchen is equipped with a rectangular frying pan, which has only one purpose: to make rolled omelets, one of the staples of Japanese cooking. Rolled omelets are light, golden-yellow, and sweetish—they are often seasoned with sugar. In a sushi shop, connoisseurs always try the rolled omelet first. If it is moist, delicately flavored, and not too sweet, the chef knows his job. Added to which, the omelet is said to "season" the stomach and make it ready for the richness of raw fish. If you don't have a rectangular frying pan, you can make rolled omelets in a small omelet pan and trim them into rectangles. As in making any omelet, the pan needs to be hot before you pour in the egg mixture. If you have any difficulty rolling the omelet, omit the dashi. A bamboo rolling mat helps to give the roll a good shape.

SERVES 2

MAKES 1 ROLL

4 eggs	*1 teaspoon mirin*
2 tablespoons Dashi II (see page 23)	*½ teaspoon light soy sauce*
1 tablespoon sugar	*pinch salt*
	vegetable oil

PREPARATION AND COOKING Mix the eggs, dashi, sugar, mirin, soy sauce, and salt in a jug and beat lightly; the eggs should not become frothy.

Heat a rectangular or small round omelet pan over medium heat and brush lightly with oil. Pour in just enough of the egg mixture to coat the pan, tilting the pan so that the egg forms an even layer.

As soon as the mixture sets (it may still be moist on top), roll up the omelet toward you with the help of chopsticks or a spatula. Oil the pan, then push the roll to the back and oil the front of the pan. Pour in more of the egg mixture, lifting the roll so that the egg flows underneath. Cook and roll up as before, and continue until all the egg mixture is used, to make a single roll with many layers.

Lift the roll out of the pan onto a bamboo rolling mat (a clean tea towel will do as a substitute). Roll it firmly and leave it to rest for a few minutes. Then unroll and cut it across into 1-inch slices.

1 Rolled omelet: roll up the omelet toward you.

2 Push to the back of the pan.

3 Add more egg mixture; lift the roll so it can flow underneath.

TO SERVE Serve 2 or 3 slices of rolled omelet as a side dish, garnished with a sprig of parsley. Rolled omelet can be served fresh from the pan or at room temperature.

To make a particularly decorative roll, you can roll a sheet of dried nori seaweed with the omelet. Take a 7-inch square piece of nori, toast it, and cut it in half with scissors. Proceed as above, but just before each rolling, lay a half sheet of nori on top of the egg and roll them up together. Each slice of omelet will have a dark-green spiral pattern.

Marinated Tofu, Tatsuta-Style

TOFU TATSUTA-AGE

■

This is a variation of a recipe that is usually used for chicken, and is a particularly tasty way of serving tofu. Tatsuta, near the ancient city of Nara, is famous for the wonderful redness of its maple leaves in autumn. In this dish, named after the area, tofu is flavored and colored by a rich soy sauce marinade, and then fried in a crisp coating. Once the tofu has absorbed the marinade it becomes very delicate and needs to be handled with care.

SERVES 4

1½ pounds fresh tofu

¼ cup white sesame seeds, toasted and lightly ground (see page 28)

½ cup all-purpose flour

vegetable oil plus a dash of sesame oil

MARINADE

½ cup dark soy sauce

¼ cup clear honey

2 teaspoons fresh ginger juice (see page 24)

2 tablespoons sake or mirin

PREPARATION *Tofu:* Carefully cut the tofu into ½-inch slices. Spread them on several thicknesses of clean tea towels, cover with more tea towels, and set aside to drain and firm up for at least 1 hour.

Marinade: Stir together the marinade ingredients and pour into a wide shallow platter. Lay the prepared tofu slices in a single layer in the marinade and leave for another hour, spooning over the marinade from time to time. Then turn them—very carefully—to marinate the other side for another hour.

TO COOK Mix together the sesame seeds and flour. Heat a little oil in a frying pan. Carefully lift a few of the tofu slices from the marinade and dip them in the flour mixture to coat both sides. Fry them, a few at a time, for 2-3 minutes on each side over medium heat until the coating is crisp and brown. Repeat with the remaining slices of tofu.

Pour the remaining marinade into a small saucepan and boil it over high heat for 2-3 minutes so that it reduces and thickens slightly.

TO SERVE Serve immediately on individual plates, topped with a little of the reduced marinade.

Baked Dishes

■

Sea Bass Baked in Foil

SUZUKI GINGAMI-YAKI

■

One of the most delicious ways of cooking fish is to parcel it up tightly and bake it in the oven, so that it steams in its own juices and none of the flavor or goodness is lost. In the distant past, the Japanese used bamboo leaves. Nowadays aluminum foil makes a very convenient alternative. Any filleted white fish—sea bream, flounder, sole—or salmon or trout are all good cooked in this way.

SERVES 4

1 12-ounce fillet sea bass

salt

8 fresh button mushrooms, wiped

*8 gingko nuts, fresh or canned
(if available)*

vegetable oil

*4 ounces uncooked medium shrimp,
shelled*

soy sauce

MARINADE

*1 teaspoon fresh ginger juice
(see page 24)*

2 tablespoons sake

1 teaspoon soy sauce

PREPARATION *Sea bass:* Cut the sea bass into 4 pieces. Put them into a large strainer, skin side down, and sprinkle with a little salt. Set aside for 30 minutes.

Vegetables: Cut off and discard the mushroom stalks; cut a neat cross in the top of each cap. Shell, boil, and peel fresh gingko nuts; drain canned nuts.

Marinade: Mix the marinade ingredients. Rinse the sea bass pieces well, pat them dry with paper toweling, and lay them in a shallow dish. Pour over the marinade and set aside for 10 minutes.

Preheat the oven to 375°F. Cut four 12-inch squares of aluminum foil and brush with oil. Drain the fish, reserving the marinade, and put a piece of fish, skin side up, in the middle of each piece of foil. Arrange a few shrimp, 2 mushrooms, and 2 gingko nuts (if using) on each piece of fish and sprinkle with the reserved marinade. Fold the foil up and around the fish carefully to make a parcel, twisting the edges tightly together to make a close seal.

TO COOK Put the parcels on a baking sheet and bake for 15–20 minutes, until the fish flakes easily when tested with a fork (test by opening one package slightly; reseal, and continue cooking if necessary).

TO SERVE Put each parcel on a small plate and serve unopened, with salt and soy sauce; there is a wonderful aroma when the parcels are opened.

STEAMED DISHES

Mushimono

Some of the most visually beautiful dishes in the Japanese repertoire are steamed. The various ingredients are assembled on the plate almost like a still life, then carefully put into the steamer without disturbing the arrangement, and finally served up just as they are, with the colors all dewy-bright from steaming.

Steamed dishes are more part of the culinary tradition in Asian countries—Japan, China, Korea—than in the West, although here, too, people are finally becoming aware that steaming is one of the very healthiest ways to cook food. Steaming locks in all the flavor and goodness of the food and keeps it moist and tender, as well as preserving the shape and enhancing the color. It is a particularly appropriate technique for fish and vegetables; chicken is also very popular cooked this way.

Most kitchens in Japan are furnished with a steamer, either a stacking bamboo one, like the ones in Chinese restaurants, or, more usually, a metal steamer with holes in the bottom. In the past, Western kitchens, too, had steamers, like a double boiler with holes in the bottom of the top pan. A large traditional steamer is best for Japanese dishes; otherwise it is fairly simple to improvise. (A collapsing vegetable steamer will *not* do.)

To improvise, you will need a large heavy saucepan and some kind of support inside it on which to stand the dish or plate of food. A rack or colander, or a heat-proof bowl turned upside-down, will be fine. Make sure that there is plenty of water in the saucepan and that the dish of food is well above it. To prevent condensation from dropping on the cooking food, stretch a clean tea towel under the lid.

Always put foods into a hot steamer with a good head of steam. Apart from eggs, most foods are steamed over high heat, for as short a time as possible.

Sake-Steamed Sole

KAREI NO SAKAMUSHI

∎

Steaming is an ideal method for cooking fish. Besides sole, sea bass and salmon are good cooked this way.

SERVES 4

4 fillets petrale or lemon sole	SAUCE
3-inch square dried kombu seaweed	*1 cup dashi (see page 22)*
3 tablespoons sake	*¼ teaspoon salt*
salt	*½ teaspoon light soy sauce*
1 bunch garden cress or watercress sprigs	*1 tablespoon ground kuzu or cornstarch*
1 lemon, cut into wedges	*½ teaspoon freshly squeezed lemon juice*

PREPARATION Cut the fillets into wide strips. Wipe the kombu, cut it into fourths, and lay a piece in the bottom of each of 4 small, deep, heatproof bowls. Put the fish on top and sprinkle with sake and a little salt. Cover the bowls with aluminum foil or plastic wrap.

Divide the cress into 4 bunches of 5 to 6 sprigs each. Holding each bunch with chopsticks, dunk it in boiling water until wilted. Set aside on paper toweling to drain.

TO COOK Put the bowls into a preheated steamer and steam over high heat for 6 minutes, until the sole is cooked; it should flake easily when tested with a fork.

Meanwhile, make the sauce: Mix the dashi, salt, and soy sauce in a saucepan and bring to a simmer. Dissolve the kuzu in 1 tablespoon water. Add it to the mixture and stir until thickened. Remove from the heat and stir in the lemon juice.

TO SERVE Lift the bowls out, remove their lids, and spoon the sauce over. Lay a bunch of cress in each bowl as a garnish and serve with lemon wedges on the side.

Sake-Steamed Chicken with A Lemony Sauce

TORI NO SAKAMUSHI

■

In this recipe chicken is steamed with mushrooms and lemon slices and served with ponzu, a tangy lemon-based sauce. The sauce can be made in some quantity and stored in the refrigerator for up to 3 months. It can also be bought ready-made.

SERVES 4

PONZU SAUCE

½ cup freshly squeezed lemon juice

½ cup dark soy sauce

¼ cup mirin

2 tablespoons rice vinegar

2 tablespoons dashi (see page 22)

handful dried bonito flakes

*2 chicken thighs, boned but
  not skinned*

sake

salt

vegetable oil

*4 dried shiitake mushrooms, soaked
  in water until soft*

½ lemon

GARNISHES

grated daikon radish (see page 21)

seven spice pepper

1 green onion

PREPARATION AND COOKING *Ponzu sauce:* Mix all the ingredients and leave for 24 hours. Decant or strain, leaving behind the bonito flakes, just before use.

Chicken: Lay the chicken on a cutting board and pierce the skin with a fork several times. Sprinkle it with sake and salt. Heat a little oil in a frying pan and flash fry the chicken to seal in the juices; set aside to cool slightly.

Mushrooms: Drain, then cut off and discard the mushroom stalks; cut the caps into thin slices.

Lemon: Slice the lemon thinly.

TO COOK Slice the chicken and lay the slices alternately with the mushrooms in a heatproof bowl or baking pan. Put the lemon slices on top, and sprinkle with salt. Cover with aluminum foil and steam in a preheated hot steamer for 20 minutes.

While the chicken is steaming, prepare the garnishes: Sprinkle the grated daikon with seven spice pepper and squeeze it to make 4 mounds. Slice the green onion very finely into rounds, rinse it in cold water, and squeeze it to drain.

TO SERVE Choose 4 attractive serving plates and divide the chicken slices, mushrooms, and lemon slices among them. Pour the ponzu into 4 small bowls and put a small mound of daikon and some green onion slices in each.

Sea Bream Steamed Shinshu-Style

TAI NO SHINSHU-MUSHI

ILLUSTRATED ON PAGE 78

This beautiful dish is a work of art, with brown noodles looped gracefully around a piece of fish. The Japanese sea bream (sold as "Tai snapper") is imported from Australia. Red snapper or porgy are alternatives.

SERVES 4

1 sea bream, filleted in half

salt

4 large dried shiitake mushrooms, soaked in water until soft

½ cup dashi (see page 22)

2 teaspoons dark soy sauce

SAUCE

¾ cup dashi (see page 22)

6 teaspoons sake

1 green onion

4 ounces soba buckwheat noodles

4 small pieces dried kombu seaweed, wiped

4 teaspoons mirin

4 teaspoons dark soy sauce

handful dried bonito flakes

PREPARATION *Sea bream:* Rinse the fillets and pat dry. Take one fillet and cut 2 slices, each 2 inches wide, from the center. Do the same with the remaining fillet. Take one of these slices and make a horizontal cut from the thin side to the thick side (i.e. towards the center of the fish), so that the slice opens out like a book. Repeat with the remaining slices.

Mushrooms: Drain the mushrooms. Cut off and discard the hard stalks; cut the caps in half. Simmer the mushroom caps in the dashi, soy sauce, and 2 teaspoons sake for 15–20 minutes; top up the simmering liquid with more dashi as necessary. Leave to cool in the cooking liquid, then drain well.

Green onion: Shred the green onion as finely as possible. Rinse it in cold water, drain, and pat dry.

Noodles: Separate the noodles into 4 bunches and tie each bunch firmly at the base with sewing cotton or a rubber band. Cook in plenty of rapidly boiling salted water for 5–7 minutes until the noodles are *al dente*. Drain them and put them straight into cold water to stop the cooking process, then drain again.

Take 1 piece of fish and lay it on a cutting board skin side up. Open it out then close it around one end of a bunch of noodles and fold the noodles over the fish; cut off the end tied with string. Repeat with the remaining 3 pieces of fish.

Choose 4 attractive heatproof bowls. In each lay a piece of kombu, then the fish wrapped with noodles, and a couple of mushroom pieces. Sprinkle 1 teaspoon of sake over each piece of fish. Cover the bowls tightly with aluminum foil.

TO COOK Put the bowls into a preheated steamer and steam for 10 minutes over high heat. Meanwhile, make the sauce.

Sauce: Bring the dashi, mirin, and soy sauce to the boil in a small saucepan. Toss in the bonito flakes, give the mixture a stir, and strain it immediately through muslin or a fine strainer. Discard the bonito flakes.

TO SERVE Lift the bowls out of the steamer, remove the foil, and ladle the hot sauce over. Garnish with a mound of shredded green onion and serve immediately.

Chicken Steamed in Foil

TORI MUSHI-YAKI

In this dish chicken is steamed in its own juices, without any added liquid. The Japanese word *mushi-yaki* means "steam-grilled."

SERVES 4

*2 chicken breasts, boned but
  not skinned*

*12 fresh shiitake mushrooms
  or large cultivated mushrooms,
  wiped*

1 teaspoon salt

20 gingko nuts, fresh or canned

1 tablespoon sake

1 lemon, cut into wedges

SAUCE

¼ cup sake

*1 cup grated daikon radish
  (see page 21)*

4 green onions, shredded

½ cup soy sauce

*2 tablespoons freshly squeezed
  lemon juice*

¼ teaspoon seven spice pepper

PREPARATION Cut the chicken into bite-sized pieces. Cut off and discard the mushroom stalks; cut the caps into quarters. Sprinkle both chicken and mushrooms with salt. Shell, boil, and peel fresh gingko nuts; drain canned nuts. Sprinkle the sake over the chicken, mushrooms, and gingko nuts and set aside.

Cut four 12-inch squares of aluminum foil. Divide the chicken, mushrooms, and gingko nuts among the foil pieces. Fold the foil up and around the chicken carefully to make parcels, twisting the edges tightly together to make a close seal.

TO COOK Put the parcels into a preheated steamer and steam for 15-20 minutes over high heat until the chicken is cooked.

Meanwhile, mix the sauce ingredients together. If preferred, burn off the alcohol in the sake first: put it into a small saucepan, heat it, then remove, ignite with a long-handled match, and shake the pan gently until the flame dies out. Allow it to cool before mixing with the other ingredients.

TO SERVE Open the parcels and serve with lemon wedges and sauce for dipping.

Savory Steamed Custard-in-a-Cup

CHAWAN MUSHI

■

ILLUSTRATED ON PAGE 79

Chawan mushi (literally "steamed cup") is so popular that the Japanese have developed cups specially for it—small porcelain ones with matching lids. Eating it is a bit like a treasure hunt. With your spoon (you are allowed to use a spoon, unusual for Japanese cuisine) you dig into the delicate savory custard and unearth all kinds of treasures—gingko nuts, nuggets of chicken, pink prawns, shiitake mushrooms. The exact contents depend on the cook.

If you don't have *chawan mushi* cups, it looks very attractive served in a coffee cup, custard bowl, or ramekin, with aluminium foil as a lid.

SERVES 4

3-4 ounces chicken breast,
    boned and skinned

1 teaspoon sake

1 teaspoon light soy sauce

4 medium uncooked prawns in shell

salt

2 fresh shiitake mushrooms
    (or 4 cultivated mushrooms),
    wiped

8 gingko nuts, fresh or canned
    (optional)

4 lemon zest "twists" (see page 41)

4 sprigs fresh coriander, washed and
    patted dry

CUSTARD

5 cups dashi (see page 22)

1 tablespoon sake

1 tablespoon light soy sauce

½ teaspoon salt

3 eggs (see page 31)

PREPARATION *Chicken:* Cut the chicken into 1-inch cubes. Sprinkle it with the sake and soy sauce and leave it to marinate for about 15 minutes.

Prawns: Shell and devein the prawns, leaving the last tail section intact. Sprinkle them with a little salt. If they are very big, cut them in half lengthways.

Shiitake mushrooms: Cut off and discard the stalks; cut the caps into halves or quarters.

Gingko nuts: If you can find fresh gingko nuts, shell, boil, and peel them. Drain canned nuts.

Custard: Mix the dashi with the sake, soy sauce, and salt and heat slightly; it should be warm but not hot. Mix the eggs very lightly so that they do not become frothy, and stir in the warm dashi mixture.

Arrange the solid ingredients in 4 heatproof cups, filling them not more than three-quarters full. Ladle over the custard mixture, leaving at least ½ inch clear at the top of each cup, and float a lemon "twist" and a sprig of coriander on each. Cover each cup with a lid or aluminum foil.

TO COOK Put the 4 cups into a preheated steamer and steam gently for 13-15 minutes, until the custard is just set; it will still be very soft. (Insert a wooden toothpick to check if the custard is set; the toothpick should come out clean.)

TO SERVE Serve the *chawan mushi* immediately in its cup, with a spoon.

Egg "Tofu"

TAMAGO-DOFU

This is actually not tofu at all, but a block of very light savory custard, pale yellow and delicately flavored, which is served chilled in summer.

It takes a little care in the making. The Japanese use a small square pan with a removable base, a *yokan* pan (normally used to make *yokan,* aduki bean jelly). To improvise, line a straight-sided square or oblong pan—such as a 1-pound loaf pan—with aluminum foil, making it as smooth as possible. Cook the custard over very low heat, so that it does not puff up or bubble, and take it off the heat as soon as it is set.

SERVES 4

4 eggs	SAUCE
1 cup dashi (see page 22)	*½ cup dashi (see page 22)*
2 tablespoons mirin	*1½ tablespoons light soy sauce*
2 tablespoons light soy sauce	*1½ tablespoons mirin*
¼ teaspoon salt	*2 tablespoons dried bonito flakes*
4 sprigs fresh coriander, washed and patted dry	

PREPARATION AND COOKING Beat the eggs thoroughly, then gently stir in the dashi, mirin, soy sauce, and salt.

Line a small square baking pan or 1-pound loaf pan with aluminum foil, as smoothly as possible. Pour in the egg mixture to a depth of 1½-2 inches; the pan should be no more than two-thirds full. Lightly cover the top of the pan with foil.

Steam in a preheated steamer for 4 minutes over high heat; then reduce the heat to low and steam until a wooden toothpick inserted in the custard comes out clean and the custard is just set (20-30 minutes). There will be a little free dashi around the custard.

Put the pan in cold water. Run a knife around the edge to loosen the custard and cut it into 4 pieces, then either remove the sides of the pan or gently lift out the foil lining. Put a plate over the egg "tofu" and invert it onto the plate. Ease away the pan base or foil and refrigerate to cool.

Sauce: Mix the sauce ingredients in a small saucepan, bring to the boil, then cool to room temperature. Strain.

TO SERVE Choose 4 small glass bowls. Put a "tofu" cube in each bowl, with the top, smooth side uppermost. Spoon a little sauce over each, lay a sprig of coriander on top, and serve.

DEEP-FRIED DISHES

Agemono

Deep-frying is a serious business in Japan. The very best tempura, for example, is produced in restaurants that serve nothing else, where the chefs spend all day long making only tempura. Tempura restaurants are sober, modest places, with a stripped pine counter where a row of customers sit on stools, watching intently while the maestro turns out perfectly deep-fried morsels of seafood and vegetables, coated in the lightest, frothiest of batters, and arranges them like a miniature landscape on a plate.

Properly done, deep-fried foods are not the tiniest bit oily. In fact, deep-frying can be a very healthy way of cooking; foods are cooked in a matter of seconds, so that all the freshness and flavor are sealed in.

There are a couple of secrets that ensure perfect deep-frying. The first is the oil. The Japanese use only pure vegetable oil, never animal fats, adding a little sesame oil for flavor (up to 1 part sesame oil to 2 parts vegetable oil). For the most delicate dishes it is essential to use oil that is clean, pure, and unused, though for other dishes it is possible to reuse the oil a few times. It is said that the very best tempura restaurants use only the freshest oil, then sell their once-used oil to the next best restaurant, which uses it and sells it to the next best, and so on down the line—a story that may discourage you from eating cheap tempura!

The second secret is the temperature of the oil. It must be kept high and even. You can check it with a deep-frying thermometer or use the batter test: drop a little batter or a tiny piece of bread into hot oil. At 350°F, the usual deep-frying temperature, it will sink then rise quickly to the surface. If it sizzles on the surface, the oil is too hot; if it sinks to the bottom and stays there, the oil is too cold.

Always deep-fry in plenty of oil and cook only a few items at a time; if the pan is too full, the temperature of the oil will drop. Deep-fried foods are always served immediately (after being drained for a few seconds on paper toweling). They are usually accompanied with a delicately flavored sauce.

Deep-Fried Sole

KAREI KARA AGE

■

Sole fillets are delicious dusted with kuzu and simply deep-fried.

SERVES 4

4 fillets sole

salt

kuzu (or flour or cornstarch)

vegetable oil plus a little sesame oil

*4-inch length daikon radish,
    peeled and grated*

1 lemon, cut into wedges

DIPPING SAUCE

1 cup dashi (see page 22)

3 tablespoons mirin

3 tablespoons soy sauce

handful dried bonito flakes

PREPARATION *Sole:* Lay the fillets on a cutting board with the dark side upwards and cut a shallow cross in the top. Alternatively, cut the fillets into strips or into 1¼-inch squares. Sprinkle with a little salt and set aside to drain.

Dipping sauce: Bring the dashi, mirin, and soy sauce to the boil in a small saucepan. As it comes to the boil, put in the bonito flakes and remove from the heat immediately. Wait until the flakes begin to sink, and strain the sauce through muslin or a fine sieve. Keep warm.

Rinse the fish and pat dry. Grind the kuzu in a *suribachi* or mortar and pestle and coat the fillets or pieces of sole with it (alternatively use flour or cornstarch). Set aside for a few minutes so that the coating can set.

TO COOK Half fill a small heavy saucepan with 2-3 inches of vegetable oil, adding a little sesame oil for flavor. Slowly heat to 350°F and deep-fry the fillets one at a time (or deep-fry the pieces of sole 4 or 5 at a time) until golden brown and cooked through. Drain on kitchen paper or a wire rack and keep warm.

TO SERVE Line 4 plates with folded paper napkins and arrange the fish on each, together with a wedge of lemon. Serve the dipping sauce separately in 4 small bowls and put a little grated daikon into each bowl. Serve immediately.

Mixed Tempura

TEMPURA MORIAWASE

■

ILLUSTRATED ON PAGE 80

Tempura—seafoods and vegetables deep-fried in a lacy batter—is one of the great classic Japanese dishes.

In 1543 three Portuguese sailors were shipwrecked off the coast of Japan and decided to settle there. Following in their wake came a great tidal wave of missionaries, traders, and adventurers—Spanish, Portuguese, English, and Dutch. By 1640 the shogun, the ruler of the country, had had enough. He decided to bar all foreigners from the country—but not before they had had a profound effect on its cuisine.

On Ember Days, the four feast days of the Catholic calendar—the *Quattuor Tempora,* the Four Times—the Portuguese used to abstain from meat; instead they ate seafood, usually prawns, which they fried in batter. This "tempora" became tempura—though the Japanese, as always, improved on their borrowing, devising a lighter batter and cooking with a lighter oil.

Tempura is one of the most artistic of dishes, and sculpting the seafood and vegetables for deep-frying is a real pleasure. You will need time and space to make this dish. The real secret of tempura lies in the batter. Leave it until the last minute; be sure to use ice water; and—the only difficult bit—resist all temptation to beat it or overstir it. It should be barely mixed and still lumpy, pocked with lumps of dry flour.

If you can get them, Japanese noodles—somen and harusame—do quite magical things when deep-fried. Harusame blow up into wriggling prawn-cracker-like snakes, while somen softens in the hot oil and can be eased into an attractive basket shape—perfect for serving tempura in.

The following is only a sample selection of the possible vegetables and seafoods for this recipe. Practically any fish, seafood, or dry vegetable makes delicious tempura.

SERVES 4

8 uncooked prawns in shell

4 sea scallops

1 Japanese eggplant
(about 8 ounces), trimmed

1 large carrot, peeled

½ green bell pepper, deseeded

1 medium onion, peeled

8 fresh mushrooms
(shiitake or any other sort), wiped

12 green beans, topped and tailed

1 sheet dried nori seaweed,
7 × 8 inches

11-14 ounces somen egg noodles
(optional)

5 ounces harusame noodles
(optional)

vegetable oil for deep frying

sesame oil

flour for dusting

DIPPING SAUCE

1¼ cups dashi (see page 22)

¼ cup soy sauce

¼ cup mirin

CONDIMENTS

½ daikon radish, peeled

1-inch piece fresh ginger root, peeled

BATTER

2 egg yolks (see page 31)

2 cups ice water

2 cups all-purpose flour

PREPARATION *Prawns:* Shell and devein the prawns, leaving the tails on. Rinse them in salted water, then in plain water. Cut off the tips of the tails and make 3 or 4 cuts across the belly to stop them from curling up while they are frying, then tap the back of each prawn with the flat of a knife blade and squeeze gently with your fingers to get rid of some of the moisture.

Scallops: Clean the scallops and pat dry. Slice plump scallops in half crossways.

Eggplant: Cut the eggplant into thin slices or into decorative fans. To make eggplant fans, trim the eggplant and cut it across in half, then quarter each half lengthways. Take one of these segments, cut away a thin strip down the center to make a wedge shape (see illustration), then make evenly spaced cuts lengthways very close together to make the fan, leaving ½ inch at the bottom. Press down at the base to spread the fan open.

1 Eggplant fan: cut a wedge-shaped piece, then make a series of parallel cuts.

2 Gently press at the base to spread the fan open.

Mushrooms: 2 notched cuts at right angles make a decorative cross

Onion slices: keep onion slices together with a toothpick.

Carrot: Cut thin rectangles of carrot 2½ × ¾ inches. Make 2 cuts and twist to form a triangle, crossing the ends to secure (see illustration on page 41).

Green pepper: Cut into strips

Onion: Halve and cut across into slices. Insert a toothpick before you make each slice to stop the slices from falling apart into rings.

Mushrooms: Cut off and discard the stalks; notch a decorative cross in each mushroom cap (see page 111).

Green beans: Cut in half. With scissors, cut the nori seaweed in half. Cut one half into narrow strips and use it to tie the beans in groups of 3, wetting the end of the nori to seal it.

Somen noodles: The somen noodles come ready bound together into bundles. To make a somen basket, cut 2 long strips of nori, each 1 inch wide. Take ½ bundle of somen—treat it with great care—and wrap each end securely with a strip of nori, sealing the end of the nori with a little egg white, then finally remove the paper that holds the somen together.

To make somen fans, cut thin strips of nori 3-4 inches long. Remove the paper wrapping from one bundle of noodles and separate the bundle into 8 or 10 parts. Take one group of noodles and cut them in half with scissors (carefully—they are very fragile!), then wrap securely at one end with nori seaweed. Repeat until you have made 3 or 4 of these.

Harusame noodles: Separate out about 6 noodles (a bundle about the thickness of your little finger), cut them in half with scissors and bind them in the middle with thin strips of nori.

Dipping sauce: Mix the dipping sauce ingredients in a small saucepan, bring to a boil, and keep warm.

Condiments: Grate the daikon radish and the ginger separately on a very fine grater. Squeeze the daikon with your fingers and make 4 small cones (you may not need all the daikon to do this); top each cone with a little ginger like the snow cap on a mountain. Neatly fold 4 white paper napkins (not in half but asymmetrically) and place on 4 small plates; put a daikon cone on each plate.

Oil: Half fill a small heavy saucepan with 2-3 inches of vegetable oil, adding a little sesame oil for flavor. Slowly heat to 350°F.

Batter: While the oil is heating, prepare half the total recipe of batter: stir together the egg yolk and ice water very lightly with chopsticks; do not beat. Add the flour all at once and mix in very lightly; the batter will still have lumps of unmixed flour and be thick and very lumpy. Make the rest of the batter half-way through cooking: it should be made and used straight away, never left to sit.

Make sure that all the vegetables and seafood are dry and lay them out on a tray beside the cooker, together with a bowl of flour for dusting and the bowl of batter. You will also need long cooking chopsticks and a skimmer, and some paper toweling or a rack for draining the cooked tempura.

TO COOK Check the temperature of the oil before you begin frying. Dip each item first into flour, then into batter, then put it gently into the oil. Deep-fry for 1-3 minutes, turning occasionally, until both sides are crisp and turning golden. Cook only a few items at a time and make sure that they do not touch and that the pan is not crowded. From time to time skim the oil to clear away scraps of batter.

Briefly drain the cooked tempura on a rack or paper toweling before transferring to individual plates.

Somen and harusame noodles can go straight into the hot oil. To make a somen basket: as the somen softens, ease the bundle of noodles gently apart in the center with chopsticks to make a basket shape (see illustration).

Somen basket: as the noodles soften in the oil, ease them apart in the center with chopsticks.

TO SERVE Pour the dipping sauce into 4 small bowls. Arrange the tempura attractively on the folded paper on the plate; traditionally larger items go at the back with smaller ones propped against them. Serve as it is cooked, with the dipping sauce and condiments. Your guests mix the condiments into the dipping sauce and dip the tempura into it before eating.

Mixed Vegetable Pancakes

KAKI AGE

This is almost an extension of the previous recipe and an economical and delicious way to use up leftover tempura batter. It is also worth making in its own right—a sort of lazy man's tempura.

SERVES 4

2 medium carrots, peeled

1 onion, peeled

1 young leek, washed and trimmed

2 ounces green beans, topped and tailed

batter as for Mixed Tempura (see page 110)

dipping sauce and condiments as for Mixed Tempura (see page 110)

vegetable oil plus a little sesame oil for deep-frying

PREPARATION Cut all the vegetables into thin strips or pieces, about 2 inches long, and pat dry with paper toweling. Lightly mix with enough batter to coat all the ingredients. Prepare the dipping sauce and condiments.

TO COOK Half fill a small heavy saucepan with 2-3 inches of vegetable oil, adding a little sesame oil for flavor. Slowly heat to 350°F. Put spoonfuls of the vegetable mixture into the hot oil, 2 or 3 at a time, and deep-fry for about 1 minute on each side, until golden. Remove and drain on paper toweling.

TO SERVE Serve immediately, with the dipping sauce and condiments.

Marinated Chicken
Tatsuta-Style

TORINIKU TATSUTA-AGE

■

Named after the Tatsuta area, which is famous for its wonderful red maple leaves, in this recipe chicken is marinated in soy sauce until it turns a rich red-brown, then deep-fried. Fresh ginger gives a tang to the marinade.

SERVES 4

*1½ pounds boned chicken,
  thigh and breast, with skin*

12 green beans, topped and tailed

*vegetable oil plus a little sesame oil
  for deep frying*

cornstarch

1 lemon, cut into wedges

MARINADE

¼ cup sake

¼ cup dark soy sauce

1 tablespoon sugar

*1 tablespoon fresh ginger juice
  (see page 24)*

*1 tablespoon crushed or finely
  chopped garlic (optional)*

PREPARATION Cut the chicken into large bite-sized pieces. Mix the marinade ingredients in a bowl, add the chicken and leave it to marinate for 20-30 minutes.

Meanwhile, prepare the beans: Cook them in rapidly boiling water for 1-2 minutes, until they are just tender, then refresh in cold water, drain, pat dry, and set aside.

TO COOK Half fill a small saucepan with 2-3 inches of oil, adding a little sesame oil for flavor. Slowly heat to 350°F.

Meanwhile, drain the chicken pieces and toss them in cornstarch. Shake off the excess and set them aside for a few minutes for the coating to set. Deep-fry, a few at a time, for about 4-5 minutes until crisp and brown. Drain on paper toweling and keep warm in the oven until all the chicken is cooked.

TO SERVE Fold 4 white paper napkins and place on 4 plates. Divide the chicken between the plates, garnish each plate with 3 beans and a slice of lemon and serve.

Deep-Fried Tofu in Broth

AGEDASHI DOFU

This is the most classic of tofu dishes, almost a celebration of it. It is just tofu, plain and simple—cut into blocks, deep-fried until it is pale gold, and served with the most delicate of sauces to accentuate the flavor.

SERVES 4

12 ounces fresh tofu	*1 green onion, washed and trimmed*
finely ground kuzu or cornstarch	*2 packets (0.175 ounce each)*
vegetable oil plus a little sesame oil	*dried bonito flakes*
for deep-frying	SAUCE
GARNISHES	*¼ cup dashi (see page 22)*
4-inch length daikon radish, peeled	*¼ cup soy sauce*
1-inch piece fresh ginger root, peeled	*¼ cup mirin*

PREPARATION *Tofu:* To drain the tofu, wrap it in clean tea towels, set a chopping board on top for a weight, and set aside for 30 minutes; it is best to leave it on a sloping board over the sink, as quite a lot of water will come out.

While the tofu is draining, prepare the garnishes and sauce.

Garnishes: Grate the daikon and ginger separately on a very fine grater. Squeeze to make 4 cones of daikon and 4 cones of ginger; set the remaining grated daikon aside. Slice the green onion into threads and leave to soak in cold water. Put the bonito flakes in a bowl.

Sauce: Mix the sauce ingredients together in a saucepan and bring to a simmer.

When the tofu is well drained, cut it in half and half again and, if you like, into half again, to make either 4 or 8 cubes. Roll each piece in kuzu or cornstarch and set aside.

TO COOK Half fill a small heavy saucepan with 2-3 inches of vegetable oil, adding a little sesame oil for flavor. Slowly heat to 350°F. Deep-fry the tofu piece by piece for 2½ minutes, until pale gold. Put the cooked tofu cubes to drain on paper toweling.

Remove the sauce from the heat and stir in a few spoonfuls of grated daikon. Drain the green onion slices and pat dry.

TO SERVE Choose small deep bowls; in Japan porcelain bowls with lids are used. Put 1 large or 2 small cubes of tofu in each bowl and ladle over the hot sauce. Sprinkle with green onion slices, add a pinch of bonito flakes, a cone of ginger, and a small mound of grated daikon. Serve immediately.

SIMMERED DISHES

Nimono

Simmering is surely one of the most venerable of cooking techniques. Ever since man settled down and began to make fireproof containers—clay pots, iron cauldrons—he has boiled food in water, to which he adds various flavorings.

In Japan every meal always includes a simmered dish, beginning with the simplest home meal of "soup plus three" (sashimi, a grilled dish, and a simmered dish). Halfway through a banquet, the waitresses will bring a trayful of rather large and exquisite porcelain bowls, covered with lids. They set one at each place, and there is a moment of pleasant anticipation before you lift the lid to discover a tiny landscape of beautifully sculpted vegetables brilliantly colored and meltingly soft and sweet.

Simmered dishes range from meat and fish dishes that are almost a meal in themselves, to vegetable dishes that are served, always in tiny portions, as a side dish. There are many different ways and categories of simmering, depending on the combination of ingredients used to flavor the simmering stock. For the stock itself you should properly use Dashi I (see pages 22-3), although at home people often use Dashi II (see page 23) or instant dashi. The main flavoring ingredients are sake, mirin (for which you could substitute sugar), salt, soy sauce, and miso, usually added in that order. In theory it is impossible to simmer food without a flat wooden drop lid, which floats directly on the simmering liquid, holding in the heat. But in practice I have found that an ordinary lid used in the normal way will do.

Sole Simmered in Sake

KAREI NITSUKE

■

ILLUSTRATED ON PAGE 79

Sake-simmering is one of the classic ways of cooking fish in Japan, and results in a luscious tender fish served in a sweet rich sauce. In Japan very small and tender flounder are cooked this way and served whole. In America, flounder is often marketed as "sole," even though it is not related to the true European sole. The small varieties of flounder—rex sole, sand dabs, plaice—are well suited to this dish. Or you may use fillets of larger flounder, such as lemon sole (winter flounder), fluke (summer flounder), or the delectable petrale sole. Japanese sea bream (Tai snapper) is also good cooked this way.

SERVES 4

4 small whole fish (rex sole, sand dabs, plaice), pan dressed, or 2 large fillets (about 12 ounces each; lemon sole, fluke, or petrale sole)

6 ounces spinach leaves, washed and trimmed

salt

SIMMERING STOCK

½ cup sake

½ cup mirin

¾ cup Dashi II (see page 23)

6 tablespoons dark soy sauce

2 tablespoons light soy sauce

1-2 tablespoons sugar

PREPARATION *Whole fish:* Make sure the fish is scaled and gutted—ready for cooking. Lay the fish on a cutting board with the dark side up and make a couple of diagonal slashes or a cross with a sharp knife, cutting through the skin to the central bone. This makes the fish look attractive when served and helps it to absorb the simmering liquid evenly.

Fillets: Cut each fillet in half crossways and make 2 diagonal cuts or a cross on the top side of each, as for the whole fish.

Spinach: Cook the spinach in rapidly boiling salted water for 30 seconds to 1 minute, until it is wilted and bright green, then plunge it into cold water to keep the color. Arrange the leaves neatly on a bamboo rolling mat and roll tightly to remove excess water. Set aside for a few minutes, then gently unroll from the mat and cut into 1-inch lengths.

TO COOK Use a lidded saucepan large enough to lay the fish side by side, without overlapping. First put in the sake and mirin. Bring them nearly to the boil, then remove from the heat and ignite with a long-handled match to burn off the alcohol. Shake the pan gently until the flame dies down. Add the dashi, soy sauces, and sugar and bring this stock back to the boil. (If you are worried about igniting the alcohol, simply mix all the stock ingredients together and bring to a simmer.)

Lay the fish, dark side uppermost, in a single layer in the pan. Cover with a drop lid (an ordinary lid will do), bring back to the boil, reduce the heat, and simmer over medium heat for 2 minutes. Baste the fish (do not turn it over) and simmer for another 2-3 minutes, basting frequently, until it flakes easily when tested with a fork.

TO SERVE Carefully lift the fish out of the simmering stock and arrange on shallow individual dishes. Pour over a little of the simmering stock and garnish with a slice of rolled spinach. Serve hot or at room temperature.

Mackerel Simmered in Miso

SABA MISO-NI

◼

This is one of the most popular ways of serving mackerel—simmered in a savory stock flavored with miso and ginger.

SERVES 4

4 mackerel fillets, with skin, about 4 ounces each

1 tablespoon salt

2 small leeks, washed and trimmed

¾-inch piece fresh ginger root, peeled

¾ cup dashi (see page 22)

2 tablespoons sake

1 tablespoon mirin

1 teaspoon sugar

2 tablespoons red miso

PREPARATION *Mackerel:* Rinse the fillets in cold water and pat dry. Put them in a sieve and sprinkle with the salt, then set them aside to drain for 30 minutes to 1 hour. Rinse off the salt and pat dry, then cut each fillet into 3 or 4 pieces.

Leeks: Cut the leeks into chunks. Cook them in rapidly boiling salted water for 4-5 minutes until cooked; drain.

Ginger: Slice half the ginger into paper-thin slices and set aside in cold water. Cut the remaining half into threads and poach in boiling water for a few minutes, then drain, pat dry, and set aside.

TO COOK Arrange the mackerel pieces in a single layer in a frying pan or large saucepan and lay the ginger slices on top. Pour over enough dashi to cover and add the sake, mirin, and sugar. Cover with a drop lid (or an ordinary lid). Bring to the boil, reduce the heat, and simmer over low heat until the fish is firm and flakes easily when tested with a fork. This should take 3-4 minutes. As soon as the fish is done, remove it from the heat.

TO SERVE Lift out the fish slices, arrange them in individual serving dishes, and keep warm while you make the miso sauce.

Mash the miso in a small bowl with a fork or whisk. Strain in a little of the hot simmering stock and blend it together. Pour the miso mixture back into the stock, bring it to the boil, and simmer over very low heat for a couple of minutes until the sauce is thick and glossy.

Pour the miso sauce over the fish and put some pieces of leek on each plate. Garnish with a few ginger threads and serve.

Golden Prawns

EBI KIMI-NI

Visually a very pretty dish, golden prawns are made by dredg-
ing prawns in cornstarch, then dipping them in egg yolk to
make a golden glaze. Use only large, gray, uncooked prawns.
Cooked pink ones will not do.

SERVES 4

8 large uncooked prawns in shell	SIMMERING STOCK FOR PRAWNS
salt	*2½ cups Dashi II (see page 23)*
3-4 tablespoons cornstarch	*3 tablespoons sake*
12 green beans, topped and tailed	*6 tablespoons mirin*
4 egg yolks (see page 31), well beaten	*¼ cup light soy sauce*
shreds lemon zest	

PREPARATION *Prawns:* Shell and devein the prawns, leaving the tail intact, then
rinse and pat dry. Slit open the back of each and press it out flat. If you like you
can twist them into flowers (see page 43), or simply score the flesh a couple of
times to keep it flat. Salt the prawns lightly and brush them with cornstarch to
coat evenly.

Beans: Cut the beans in half and parboil them in lightly salted water for 2-3
minutes. Drain quickly, rinse in cold water, then drain again and set aside.

TO COOK Combine the simmering stock ingredients for the prawns in a medium
saucepan and bring to the boil. Reduce heat. Holding the prawns carefully by
their tails, dip them into egg yolk, then put them into the gently simmering
stock. Simmer over low heat for 2 minutes, until the egg has set and the prawn
tails are bright pink.

TO SERVE Choose deep bowls, preferably with a lid. Arrange two prawns in each
bowl, ladle over a little of the simmering stock and place the beans alongside.
Garnish with shreds of lemon zest.

Chicken Simmered with Vegetables

UMANI

■

ILLUSTRATED ON PAGE 78

This is one of the most popular and appealing of simmered dishes—small portions of chicken and vegetables, a mouthful each. It is often served at New Year's or as part of the *makunouchi bento,* an entire lunch of different dishes, arranged in the many compartments of a beautiful lacquerware box. The word *umani* refers to the process of simmering in a fairly sweet stock. Practically any seasonal vegetable can be used in this dish.

SERVES 4

4 dried shiitake mushrooms, soaked in water until soft

SIMMERING INGREDIENTS FOR MUSHROOMS

1 cup dashi (see page 22)

1 tablespoon sake

1 tablespoon dark soy sauce

1 tablespoon sugar

4 ounces boned chicken breasts or thigh, with skin

SIMMERING INGREDIENTS FOR CHICKEN

½ cup dashi (see page 22)

3 tablespoons soy sauce

2 tablespoons mirin

8 small new potatoes, scrubbed

1 medium to large carrot, peeled

1 canned bamboo shoot

12 snow peas or green beans, topped and tailed

SIMMERING INGREDIENTS FOR VEGETABLES

2 cups dashi (see page 22)

4 teaspoons light soy sauce

1½ tablespoons mirin

1 tablespoon sugar

pinch salt

PREPARATION AND COOKING *Mushrooms:* Drain the mushrooms. Cut off and discard the stalks; cut a decorative cross in each mushroom cap (see page 111). Put the caps into a small saucepan with the dashi, sake, soy sauce, and sugar. Simmer over low heat for 20 minutes, until the mushrooms are cooked and most of the stock is absorbed; you may have to top up with a little more dashi. Leave the mushrooms to cool in the stock.

Chicken: Cut the chicken into bite-sized pieces. Put the simmering ingredients into a saucepan, add the chicken and simmer for about 5 minutes until it is cooked through and tender. Drain and set aside.

Vegetables: First make potato hexagons: trim the potatoes to make 8 thick cylinders, all about the same size. Trim the top and bottom of each cylinder to make it flat, then pare the sides neatly to make a hexagon (see illustration).

Potato hexagon: pare the sides of the potato cylinder evenly to make a hexagon.

Make 12 carrot flowers (see page 39). Parboil the potatoes and carrots in lightly salted water for 5 minutes or until half cooked; drain. Cut the bamboo shoot in half lengthways, then across into ½-inch slices.

Cook the snow peas or beans in lightly salted boiling water until they are just tender. Refresh in cold water to fix the color, then drain.

Mix the simmering ingredients for the vegetables in a medium saucepan. Add the potatoes, carrots, and bamboo shoots, bring to the boil then simmer for 20-30 minutes, until they are very well cooked and soft. Test to see how well they are done from time to time with a skewer. Drain the vegetables, reserving the stock.

TO SERVE Choose 4 deep bowls, preferably with lids. In each bowl, make a "still life" of pieces of chicken, 1 mushroom cap, 2 potato hexagons, 3 carrot flowers, and some slices of bamboo shoot. Put the larger items at the back of the bowl and lean the smaller ones artistically against them. Finally place 3 snow peas or beans at the front of the completed arrangement. Spoon over a little of the vegetable cooking stock to make a pool at the bottom of the bowl. Cover the bowls with their lids and serve, at room temperature.

Duck in
Kuzu-Thickened Sauce

KAMO YOSHINO-NI

■

The most popular part of the duck in Japanese cooking is the breast meat, the least fatty part of the bird. In this dish it is simmered in a rich sauce, which is then thickened with kuzu (or alternatively arrowroot or cornstarch). The best kuzu of all comes from the Yoshino mountains near Kyoto; hence the name of the dish. This dish is also delicious made with chicken.

SERVES 6

1 whole duck breast (both sides
   of the breastbone), boned,
   skin left on

salt

1-inch piece fresh ginger
   root, peeled

1 tablespoon ground kuzu
   (or arrowroot or cornstarch)

SIMMERING STOCK

1 cup Dashi II
   (see page 23)

¼ cup sake

1 teaspoon sugar

½ teaspoon salt

½ teaspoon soy sauce

PREPARATION *Duck:* Cut the duck breast on the diagonal into thin slices and sprinkle lightly with salt. Blanch the slices by putting them into rapidly boiling water. As soon as the water returns to the boil, lift out the slices immediately with a slotted spoon and put them to drain on paper toweling.

    Ginger: Cut the ginger into fine slices, and cut those into threads.

TO COOK Put the dashi and sake in a saucepan and bring to the boil. Add the sugar, salt, and soy sauce, stir well and put in the duck slices and ginger threads. Lower the heat and simmer uncovered for 3–4 minutes. When the duck is cooked, remove from the simmering stock with a slotted spoon and set aside.

    Mix the kuzu in a little cold water until it is well dissolved, then, over very low heat, pour gradually into the simmering stock, stirring with a whisk. Continue to stir until the sauce thickens and becomes clear. If it seems too thick, dilute with a little more dashi or water.

TO SERVE Serve the duck in small deep bowls and ladle over the sauce.

Braised Beef with Broccoli

GYUNIKU TO BUROKORI ITAME-NI

▪

Ever since the Emperor Meiji's famous New Year's dinner, meat has been a part of the Japanese diet. But beef, in particular, is still very much a luxury and, when it *is* used, tends to be cooked very simply. In this dish it is served with Western vegetables—broccoli and button mushrooms.

Ask your butcher to cut paper-thin slices of beef for you.

SERVES 4

8 ounces boneless beef sirloin, thinly sliced

4 ounces button mushrooms, wiped and trimmed

8 ounces broccoli, washed and trimmed

salt

vegetable oil

SIMMERING STOCK

1 tablespoon each sake, rice vinegar, sesame oil, water, and sugar

PREPARATION Trim the beef and cut it into 1-inch strips. Cut the mushrooms in half. Break the broccoli into florets and parboil them in lightly salted boiling water; drain. Stir together the simmering stock ingredients.

TO COOK Heat a little oil in a large saucepan. Add the mushrooms and sauté them for 1 minute, then stir in the beef and sauté for 2-3 minutes, stirring. Add the simmering stock and bring to the boil. Turn the heat down, cover with a drop lid (or an ordinary lid), and simmer over low heat for 5-6 minutes or more, until the beef is cooked through and tender. Add the broccoli just before serving and stir it to heat it through.

TO SERVE Spoon beef, mushrooms, and broccoli into small deep bowls with lids, ladle over a little of the stock, and serve hot.

Simmered Sautéed Eggplant

NASU ITAME-NI

Eggplants are considered a summer food in Japan, partly because that is when they are at their best, and partly because rich oily foods—like eggplants—are supposed to be the best antidote to Japan's hot sultry summers. Japanese eggplants are much smaller and sweeter than the globular varieties more commonly found in the West, though both types can be cooked in this way.

SERVES 4

1 Japanese eggplant, trimmed

vegetable oil

1 cup Dashi II (see page 23)

1 tablespoon mirin

2 teaspoons sugar

2 tablespoons dark soy sauce

PREPARATION Cut the eggplant in half lengthways and score the skin on the diagonal very finely. Then cut into ½-inch slices. Put them to soak in cold water for 10 minutes, then squeeze gently to remove the bitter juices.

TO COOK Heat 2-3 tablespoons oil in a heavy saucepan or deep frying pan. Add the eggplant slices and sauté them over medium heat for 5 minutes until they are half cooked. Ladle in enough dashi to cover, then add the mirin, sugar, and soy sauce. Cover, preferably with a drop lid, bring to the boil and simmer for 10 minutes until the eggplant slices are very soft and the simmering liquid has reduced a little.

TO SERVE Choose small deep bowls. Divide the eggplant among the bowls, spoon over a little of the cooking liquid and serve, hot or at room temperature.

Simmered Daikon Radish with
Flavored Miso or Hot Sesame Sauce

FURUFUKI DAIKON

■

This is a popular winter dish—fat slices of daikon radish, simmered and served with flavored miso or a sesame-base sauce.

SERVES 4

1 daikon radish, peeled

2-inch square dried kombu seaweed, wiped

salt

tiny sprigs fresh coriander, washed and patted dry

flavored white miso (see pages 72 and 81)

HOT SESAME SAUCE

¼ cup white sesame seeds (or tahini)

2 tablespoons white miso

2 teaspoons mirin

½ teaspoon powdered English mustard

1 tablespoon dashi (see page 22)

PREPARATION AND COOKING Cut the daikon radish into 1-inch slices. Bevel the top and bottom edges. Put the kombu, the daikon slices, and enough water to cover generously into a medium-sized saucepan and add a little salt. Cover, bring to the boil, and simmer for 20-40 minutes, depending on the size of the daikon, until it is very soft and slightly translucent.

To make the sesame sauce, toast the sesame seeds (see page 28). Set some aside to use as a garnish and grind the rest in a *suribachi* or mortar and pestle until they turn into paste (or use commercial tahini). Blend in the miso, mirin, and mustard and dilute with warm dashi to give a thick creamy sauce.

TO SERVE If the daikon slices are small in diameter, serve 2 or 3 per person in small deep bowls. Top each slice with a spoonful of flavored white miso or sesame sauce and garnish with a coriander sprig and toasted sesame seeds. Serve hot.

Hijiki Simmered
with Sweet Potatoes

HIJIKI NO ITAME-NI

Besides being good for you, hijiki is one of the tastiest seaweeds with an interesting chewy texture. It is frequently used in the mixed vegetable dishes that are served as side dishes at home.

SERVES 4

3 tablespoons dried hijiki seaweed

8 ounces sweet potato, scrubbed

1 tablespoon vegetable oil

1 teaspoon light soy sauce

1 teaspoon sugar

1 teaspoon sake or mirin

2 tablespoons sesame seeds, toasted (see page 28)

PREPARATION Break the hijiki into short lengths if necessary and put it into water to soak for a few minutes. Cut the sweet potato into matchsticks, immerse briefly in cold water, then drain and pat dry on paper toweling.

TO COOK Drain the hijiki, reserving the soaking water. Heat the oil in a medium saucepan and sauté the hijiki for 1-2 minutes, then add the sweet potatoes and sauté for another couple of minutes.

Measure out ½ cup of the reserved soaking water, mix it with the soy sauce, sugar, and sake or mirin and pour it over the hijiki and sweet potato mixture. Cover the pan, preferably with a drop lid, lower the heat and simmer for about 3 minutes until the sweet potato is cooked. Uncover and cook for 2 minutes longer over medium to high heat until the liquid has completely reduced; shake the pan while you are cooking but do not stir, as this breaks up the sweet potato. Lightly mix in the sesame seeds.

TO SERVE Make small mountains of the vegetable mixture in the middle of small deep bowls, one per serving. Scatter over a few more sesame seeds and serve either hot or cold.

Simmered Mixed Vegetables

YASAI ITAME-NI

■

Until recently, fresh vegetables were scarce in wintertime, and provincial grandmothers became adept at creating appetizing dishes using dried foods like seaweeds and gourd.

SERVES 4

½ ounce dried gourd (kampyo)	vegetable oil
salt	2½ cups Dashi II (see page 23)
⅓ cup dried hijiki seaweed	3 tablespoons soy sauce
1 medium carrot, peeled	4 teaspoons sugar
1 sheet deep-fried tofu (aburage)	¼ teaspoon grated fresh ginger root

PREPARATION Rub the dried gourd with salt to soften it (see page 24). Then rinse it and leave it to soak in lukewarm water. Break the hijiki into small pieces, put it into cold water to cover, and soak for a few minutes. Cut the carrot into matchsticks.

Put the deep-fried tofu into a bowl and pour boiling water over it to wash off some of the oil. Lift it out of the bowl with chopsticks (a fork will do), leave it to drain, and when it has cooled down enough to handle, cut it into thin strips.

Rinse the softened gourd and cut it into small pieces. All the chopped ingredients should be roughly the same size.

TO COOK Put a little oil into a saucepan, add the prepared ingredients, and sauté for a few minutes. Pour in enough dashi to cover, then add the soy sauce, sugar, and ginger and mix well. Bring to the boil. Reduce the heat, cover the pan (preferably with a drop lid), and simmer for about 10 minutes, until all the ingredients are done. Uncover and boil hard until well reduced. Taste and add extra soy sauce if you wish.

TO SERVE Serve in small quantities heaped in the middle of small deep bowls, one per serving. This dish can be served hot or at room temperature.

SALADS

Sunomono To Aemono

Japanese salads can be the simplest imaginable—a single ingredient with a delicate dressing—or exotic concoctions of seafoods, seaweeds, and vegetables. They are actually quite unlike our salads. For a start, the ingredients are hardly ever raw. Vegetables are nearly always either salted or parboiled, and seafoods, meat, and fish are always cooked.

Salads are served in small portions, usually heaped in the bottom of small deep bowls, shaped into miniature mountains; it is most unaesthetic to have food spread on the sides of the dish. At the beginning of a banquet, minute portions of salad are served as hors d'oeuvres, so tiny they are literally a mouthful each. Toward the end of the banquet there is more salad, as a sort of palate freshener. At home, of course, larger portions are served; or you might serve several different types of salad at one meal. The same principle applies to the presentation—a small mountain of salad in the bowl like an island in the middle of a crater lake.

Vinegared Salads

SUNOMONO

■

Vinegared salads are served with a mild dressing based on rice vinegar diluted with dashi; there is no oil at all in the dressings.

Cucumber and Wakame Salad

KYURI TO WAKAME NO SUNOMONO

■

This salad is a classic of Japanese home cooking. The dressing is called *sanbaizu*, "three-flavored vinegar," because there are three main ingredients.

SERVES 4

½ cucumber, washed and patted dry

½ teaspoon salt

¼ ounce dried wakame seaweed

SANBAIZU DRESSING

⅔ cup Dashi II (see page 23)

½ cup rice vinegar

2 tablespoons soy sauce

1½ tablespoons sugar

PREPARATION *Cucumber:* Halve the cucumber lengthways and scrape out and discard the seeds. Cut it across into paper-thin slices and put into a bowl of water to cover. Add the salt and set aside to soak for 30 minutes, then drain and pat dry.

Wakame: Soak the wakame in lukewarm water for 10 minutes. It will swell and become a rich glossy green. Drain and plunge briefly into boiling water, then rinse in cold water to make the color more intense. Drain well and pat dry. If there is a tough stalk, cut it off. Chop the wakame into small pieces, about the same size as the cucumber slices.

Dressing: Mix the dressing ingredients in a small saucepan and bring just to the boil, stirring to dissolve the sugar. Cool to room temperature.

TO ASSEMBLE AND SERVE Mix the cucumber and wakame and spoon over enough of the dressing to flavor the ingredients well and to make a small puddle at the bottom of the bowl; the vegetables should not be swimming in dressing. (Any extra dressing can be stored indefinitely in the refrigerator.) Toss gently. Choose 4 small deep bowls and arrange a mound of salad in the middle of each. Serve chilled or at room temperature.

Crab and Cucumber Salad

KANISU

■

This elegant salad is a combination of crab and cucumber with a tang of ginger. Fresh crab, of course, is best in winter. The easiest thing is to buy ready-prepared crabmeat from your fish market. White or red meat, or mixed, is fine.

SERVES 4

*6 ounces crabmeat, fresh, frozen,
    or canned*

½ cucumber, washed and patted dry

salt

*4 small lettuce leaves, washed and
    patted dry*

*1 teaspoon fresh ginger juice
    (see page 24)*

SANBAIZU DRESSING

¼ cup Dashi II (see page 23)

6 tablespoons rice vinegar

1 tablespoon light soy sauce

1 tablespoon sugar

pinch salt

PREPARATION *Crab:* For fresh crabmeat, pick it over and remove any cartilage and bits of shell. Thaw frozen crabmeat thoroughly. Rinse canned crabmeat well. Shred the prepared crabmeat finely.

Cucumber: Cut the cucumber in half lengthways and scrape out the seeds. Cut it across into paper-thin slices and put it to soak in lightly salted water for 20-30 minutes. When you are ready to use it, drain and rinse, then squeeze gently to eliminate excess water and pat dry on paper toweling.

Dressing: Mix the dressing ingredients in a small saucepan and bring just to the boil. Remove from heat and allow to cool.

TO SERVE Choose 4 glass goblets or small salad bowls and put a lettuce leaf in each. Arrange the crabmeat and cucumber on the lettuce and squeeze over a little ginger juice. Put a spoonful of dressing on each bowl and serve.

Crab and Cucumber Rolls

KANISU

■

ILLUSTRATED ON PAGE 145

This very pretty dish combines the pink of crabmeat and the green of cucumber in pale-yellow egg wrappers. It looks best served in a dark-colored bowl. Crab sticks are cylinders of compressed crabmeat or imitation crab, such as pollock. They are sold at some supermarkets and Japanese fish stores.

SERVES 4 (2 ROLLS)

8 crab sticks

4-inch length cucumber, washed and patted dry

salt

2-inch piece fresh ginger root, peeled

4 egg wrappers, made with 2 eggs and 1 egg yolk (see page 206)

a little beaten egg (see page 31)

Sanbaizu Dressing (see page 136 or 137)

PREPARATION *Crab sticks:* Cut the crab sticks in half lengthways nearly all the way through and open them out.

Cucumber: Cut the cucumber in half lengthways and scrape out the seeds. Cut it into long, transparently thin strips, the same length as the crab sticks, and soak them in lightly salted water for 20-30 minutes. When you are ready to use, drain, rinse, and pat dry on paper toweling.

Ginger: Grate half the ginger on a fine grater, and cut the remaining half into threads. Soak the threads in cold water. Drain and squeeze well before use.

TO ASSEMBLE Take a bamboo rolling mat and lay 2 egg wrappers on it with the edges overlapping well to make a continuous sheet about 7 × 8 inches. Lay 2 opened crab sticks end to end, pink side down, along the front, about 1 inch away from the edge. Arrange some cucumber slices along the crab sticks and spread a little grated ginger on top. Place 2 more crab sticks on top, pink side up.

Holding the ingredients in place with your fingers, roll the egg around them, using the bamboo mat to help firm and shape the roll. Leaving the mat behind, complete the roll; brush the edge with a little beaten egg to seal it. Set aside to rest with the sealed edge downwards.

Repeat with the remaining egg wrappers, crab sticks, and cucumber. If you have time, it is helpful to put both rolls in the refrigerator for a few hours to firm.

TO SERVE With a sharp knife, trim the ends of each roll, then cut across into 8 slices. Arrange 3 or 5 (not 4) slices in small deep dark-colored bowls. Spoon over a little dressing and decorate with a few ginger threads.

A variation is to roll each completed egg roll in a sheet of dried nori seaweed. Brush the edge with beaten egg and sauté the roll in a dry frying pan for a few seconds to seal it and toast the nori. Cut the rolls into 8 slices each and serve.

To make another sort of rolled salad, lay strips of marinated flounder, carrot, shiitake mushrooms, omelet strips, and cucumber on white kombu seaweed and roll in the same way.

Red and White Salad

KOHAKU NAMASU

This salad is always served at New Year and other holidays in Japan. Although it takes quite a long time to make, it can be prepared in quantity and keeps for up to 2 weeks in a sealed container in the refrigerator.

SERVES 4

6 ounces daikon radish, peeled

1 medium carrot, peeled

2½ teaspoons salt

1 small piece dried kombu seaweed, wiped

shreds lemon zest, soaked in cold water and squeezed dry

AMAZU DRESSING

6 tablespoons rice vinegar

6 tablespoons dashi (see page 22)

2 tablespoons sugar

PREPARATION *Daikon radish and carrot:* Cut the daikon radish and carrot into fine threads. Knead them with the salt and set aside for 30 minutes to soften.

Dressing: Combine the dressing ingredients in a small saucepan and bring just to the boil to dissolve the sugar, then set aside to cool.

Rinse the daikon and carrot and knead thoroughly until the daikon is soft and translucent, squeezing out as much liquid as possible. Measure out 3 tablespoons of the dressing and mix it with the vegetables, then knead again and discard the dressing that is pressed out.

Put the vegetables into a clean bowl; pour over the remaining dressing and mix well. Lay the dried kombu on top to give flavor, cover the bowl, and refrigerate. The salad can be served after 30 minutes, but tastes better if it is left overnight.

TO SERVE Remove the kombu. Serve very small portions, either chilled or at room temperature, and garnish with a few shreds of lemon zest.

Broccoli with Golden Dressing

BUROKORI KIMIZU

■

Golden dressing is a classic vinegar dressing thickened with egg yolks, making it rich and creamy.

SERVES 4

8 ounces broccoli, trimmed

salt

white sesame seeds, toasted (see page 28)

GOLDEN DRESSING

2 tablespoons rice vinegar (or cider vinegar)

3 tablespoons Dashi II (see page 23)

2 teaspoons mirin

2 egg yolks (see page 31)

pinch salt

PREPARATION AND COOKING *Broccoli:* Cut the broccoli into florets and parboil in lightly salted boiling water for 2-3 minutes until just tender. Refresh in cold water, then drain well and pat dry.

Golden dressing: Mix the dressing ingredients in the top of a double boiler and heat gradually, stirring continuously, until thick and creamy. Cool to room temperature.

TO SERVE Heap the broccoli in 4 deep bowls; the florets should be arranged like a mountain or a bonfire so that they don't touch the edge of the bowl. Spoon a dollop of dressing over each bowlful and sprinkle with sesame seeds to garnish.

Chrysanthemum Turnip

KIKKA KABU

◼

ILLUSTRATED ON PAGE 80

In this most famous of Japanese vegetable-cutting techniques, turnips blossom into white chrysanthemums. A steady hand and a sharp knife are required to achieve this. Chrysanthemum turnips make an attractive garnish for many dishes. The dressing is *amazu,* "sweet vinegar."

SERVES 4

4 small turnips, peeled

1 teaspoon salt

2-inch piece dried kombu seaweed, wiped

1 dried red chili pepper

AMAZU DRESSING

½ cup rice vinegar

½ cup dashi (see page 22)

2½ tablespoons sugar

PREPARATION *Turnips:* Cut a slice from the top of each turnip to make a flat base. Take 1 turnip and stand it on this base on a cutting board between 2 bamboo skewers. With a sharp knife, make a series of very fine cuts down to the skewers, then turn the turnip 90 degrees and cut again so that it is cross-hatched. Repeat with the remaining turnips.

Chrysanthemum turnip: put the turnip on a cutting board between 2 skewers and cross-hatch very finely.

Put the turnips into a bowl with the salt, kombu, and water to cover and leave them to soak for 30 minutes or until they are soft. Then rinse, drain, and gently squeeze out as much water as possible by hand.

Dressing: Combine the dressing ingredients in a small saucepan and bring just to the boil to dissolve the sugar, then set aside to cool. Take ½ the chili pepper, chop it very finely and add it to the dressing. Then pour the dressing over the prepared turnips, cover and leave them to marinate in the refrigerator for a few hours, until you are ready to use them.

TO SERVE Drain the turnips well, easing the petals apart with chopsticks. Cut 4 thin circles from the remaining chili and put 1 at the center of each flower. Serve cold or at room temperature.

To make pink chrysanthemums, divide the dressing into 2 batches and color half with red food coloring. You can also use large radishes to make very pretty chrysanthemums, with red-tinged white petals; or you can use thick slices of daikon.

Dressed Salads

AEMONO

■

Dressed salads tend to be richer and more substantial than vinegared. There are a variety of dressings, which have the consistency of mayonnaise but are made with very different ingredients. Some of the most popular use tofu, nuts, seeds, or miso, which make them nutritious and full of protein.

The first recipe in this section is for plain chilled tofu, which is not strictly a dressed salad. Tofu provides the basis for many salad dressings, and needs to be lightly drained before it is used. The simplest way is to cut it into slices and lay it on clean tea towels, with more towels on top to absorb some of the water. Or put a weight, such as a chopping board, on top and leave it for half an hour. Another method is to put the block of tofu into boiling water and let it boil for 1-2 minutes, then lift it out and use it.

A very useful piece of equipment for making dressed salads is a *suribachi* (see page 34). If you don't have one, you can grind sesame seeds with a mortar and pestle or in a food processor; or substitute tahini (commercially available sesame paste) for ground sesame seeds.

At home in Japan, dressed salads are often served directly in the *suribachi*. To do so, make the finished salad into a mound in the middle of the bowl and clean off the sides with paper toweling.

Three salads: Rolled salad in white kombu seaweed, with radish slices (page 139); Five color salad (page 155); Crab and cucumber rolls (page 138).

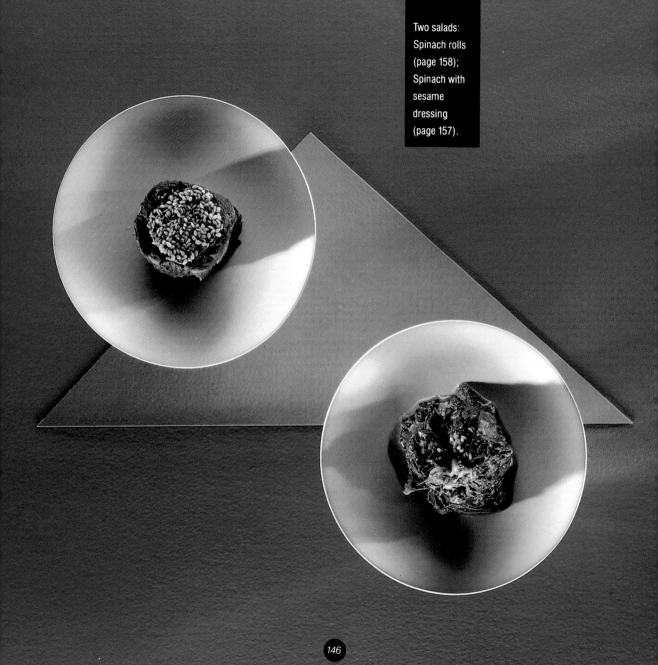

Two salads:
Spinach rolls
(page 158);
Spinach with
sesame
dressing
(page 157).

Sukiyaki: the raw ingredients ready to cook, and a raw egg for dipping (page 162).

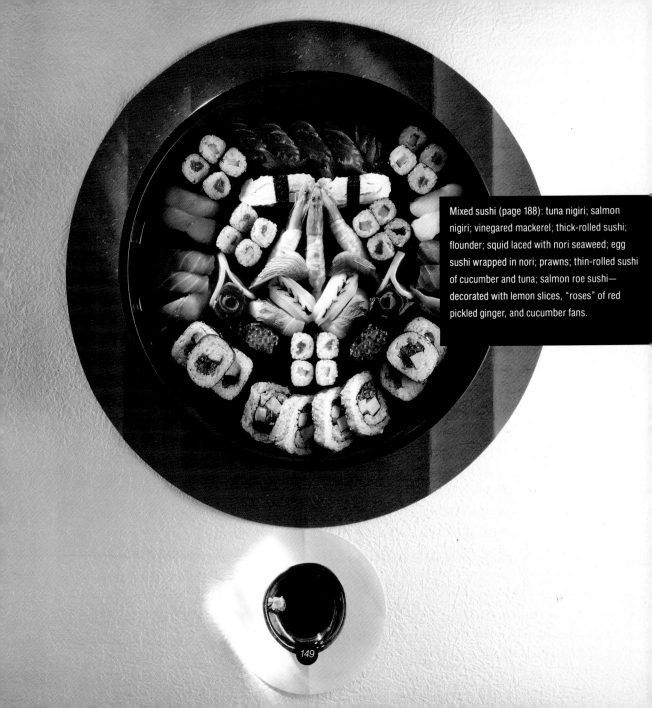

Mixed sushi (page 188): tuna nigiri; salmon nigiri; vinegared mackerel; thick-rolled sushi; flounder; squid laced with nori seaweed; egg sushi wrapped in nori; prawns; thin-rolled sushi of cucumber and tuna; salmon roe sushi—decorated with lemon slices, "roses" of red pickled ginger, and cucumber fans.

Top plate—Silk square sushi (page 206); Smoked salmon flower sushi (page 202); Smoked salmon sushi with spinach and nori seaweed (Roll-your-own-sushi, page 198). Bottom plate—nori wrapped round sushi with mustard and cress, prawns, omelet, and gourd strips; smoked salmon, salmon roe, avocado strips, and shiso leaf; tuna, squid strips, and red pickled ginger strips.

Fox noodles
(page 213);
Moon-viewing
noodles
(page 214).

A complete Japanese meal: Sea bream simmered in sake (page 120), decorated with prawns, dried shiitake mushrooms, green beans, and strips of nori seaweed; Chicken teriyaki (page 84); Crab and cucumber rolls (page 138); rice; Classic miso soup (page 45).

152

Chilled Tofu with Spicy Condiments

HIYA YAKKO

▪

For tofu *aficionados,* tofu pure and simple is the ultimate delicacy. In winter it is served hot, as *yudofu,* simmering tofu (see
page 175). In summer it is simpler still, served on a bed of ice
cubes with various contrasting flavors to accentuate the taste.

The Japanese name translates as "chilled footsoldier." The
lowest rank of samurai, the *yakko,* used to wear a uniform with
a white square, like a block of tofu, on each sleeve; so enough
tofu for one person eventually came to be known as a *yakko.*
Hiya means "chilled."

SERVES 4

1 pound fresh tofu

2 green onions

1-inch piece fresh ginger root, peeled

5 packets (0.175 ounces each)
   dried bonito flakes

dark soy sauce

PREPARATION Chill the tofu. Slice the green onions very finely, rinse in cold
water, and squeeze dry. Grate the ginger with a Japanese grater (or any other
fine-toothed grater).

TO ASSEMBLE AND SERVE Arrange the green onions, ginger, and bonito flakes
in bowls on the table and put a small bowl for dipping at each place. Cut the tofu
into 4 blocks or into small cubes and put it into 4 small glass bowls. You can sur-
round the tofu with ice cubes if you like. Serve immediately. To eat, pour a little
soy sauce into your individual dipping bowl, add condiments to taste, and dip
the tofu into the sauce first, before eating.

White Salad

SHIRA AE

∎

This is a wonderful melange of cooked vegetables with a creamy dressing of tofu and sesame seeds and is one of the staples of Japanese home cooking. If you can find *konnyaku*, it adds an interesting texture and flavor to the dish.

SERVES 4

2 medium carrots, peeled

SIMMERING STOCK FOR CARROTS

¾ cup dashi (see page 22)

1 tablespoon soy sauce

1 teaspoon sugar

1 teaspoon sake

½ block konnyaku *(optional)*

4 ounces green beans, topped and tailed

2 ounces button mushrooms, wiped

vegetable oil (optional)

toasted sesame seeds or dried nori seaweed to garnish

TOFU DRESSING

3 tablespoons sesame seeds, lightly toasted (see page 28)

8 ounces fresh tofu, drained

1 tablespoon sugar

pinch salt

PREPARATION *Carrots:* Cut the carrots into long thin strips. Put them in a saucepan with the dashi, soy sauce, sugar, and sake, bring to the boil and simmer for a few minutes until lightly cooked. Leave them to cool in the stock, then drain and set aside, reserving the cooking stock.

Konnyaku: Cut the konnyaku into strips the same size as the carrots. Parboil for 2-3 minutes, then drain and sauté in a dry pan over medium heat for 3-4 minutes, until it turns glossy and dry.

Green beans: Slice the beans on the diagonal into 1½-inch lengths and parboil; the beans should be cooked but still crisp. Drain.

Mushrooms: Cut off and discard the mushroom stalks; slice the mushroom caps. Simmer them in the reserved carrot stock, or lightly sauté them.

Dressing: Tip the toasted sesame seeds into a *suribachi* or mortar and grind until oily (or, if you like, you can use tahini, ready-ground sesame paste, instead). Add the drained tofu and grind well until the lumps have gone and the mixture is the texture of mayonnaise. Blend in the remaining dressing ingredients.

TO SERVE Just before serving, make sure that all the vegetables are perfectly dry, then mix them into the dressing. Either serve the salad in the *suribachi* (wipe down the sides with paper toweling to make it perfectly clean), or serve individual portions mounded in small deep bowls. Garnish with a sprinkling of toasted sesame seeds or a few slivers of toasted nori seaweed.

Five Color Salad

GOSHIKI NAMASU

■

ILLUSTRATED ON PAGE 145

This is a particularly rich and exotic version of White Salad.

SERVES 4

8 dried shiitake mushrooms,
 soaked in water until soft

SIMMERING STOCK
FOR MUSHROOMS

1 cup dashi (see page 22)

1 tablespoon sake or mirin

1 tablespoon sugar

1 tablespoon dark soy sauce

¼ cucumber, washed

salt

8 dried apricots

about 1 tablespoon sake

slivers lemon zest to garnish

TOFU DRESSING

2 tablespoons sesame seeds,
 lightly toasted (see page
28)

8 ounces fresh tofu, drained

1 tablespoon sugar

½ tablespoon sake or mirin

½ tablespoon rice vinegar

pinch salt

PREPARATION *Mushrooms:* Drain, then cut off and discard the mushroom stalks; slice the caps thinly. Simmer them with the dashi, sake, sugar, and soy sauce for 30 minutes, uncovered, until most of the stock is absorbed. Leave in the stock to cool, then drain.

Cucumber: Halve the cucumber lengthways and scrape out the seeds. Cut into matchsticks and put into lightly salted water to soak for 20 minutes. Rinse, drain, and pat them dry.

Apricots: Slice the dried apricots into matchsticks, sprinkle them with sake, and set aside to marinate.

Dressing: Tip the sesame seeds into a *suribachi* or mortar and grind until oily (if you like you can use tahini, ready-ground sesame paste, instead). Add the tofu and grind well until the mixture is smooth and has the texture of mayonnaise; then blend in the remaining dressing ingredients.

TO SERVE Mix the mushrooms, cucumber, and apricots into the dressing. Choose small, colorful, deep bowls and put a small mound of the salad in each. The salad should not touch the edges of the bowl. Put a few slivers of lemon zest on the top of each mound, and serve.

Spinach with Sesame Dressing

HORENSO GOMA-AE

■

ILLUSTRATED ON PAGE 146

Japanese spinach has small dark tender leaves and is sold complete with the pink root. Of the various sorts of spinach available in Western shops, the best for Japanese dishes is the small, dark-leafed variety. Cut off the bottom inch of the pink stalks, still joined together—cleaned carefully, these taste like asparagus—and save for another dish (see page 159).

SERVES 4

8 ounces spinach, washed and trimmed

salt

white sesame seeds, toasted (see page 28)

SESAME DRESSING

¼ cup white sesame seeds

1 tablespoon sugar

4 teaspoons soy sauce

1 tablespoon dashi (see page 22)

dash sake (optional)

PREPARATION *Spinach:* Blanch the spinach in lightly salted boiling water for 30 seconds to 1 minute, until the leaves turn bright green and begin to wilt. Drain immediately and plunge into cold water. Drain again and chop roughly.

Dressing: Put the sesame seeds into a *suribachi* or mortar and grind finely, then mix in the sugar and soy sauce and enough dashi to make a paste; add sake to taste. Put the spinach into the *suribachi* and toss lightly to coat with dressing.

TO SERVE Heap the spinach in the center of small deep bowls and sprinkle over a few toasted sesame seeds to garnish. Or serve the salad heaped in the middle of the *suribachi* (clean off the sides before serving).

Spinach Rolls

HORENSO GOMA-AE

ILLUSTRATED ON PAGE 146

This dish is extremely easy and visually quite delectable.

SERVES 4   (2 ROLLS)

1 pound spinach, washed

salt

¼ cup white sesame seeds

soy sauce

PREPARATION Cut off and discard the spinach stalks. Put the leaves into rapidly boiling salted water and blanch for 30 seconds to 1 minute, until they are bright green. Refresh in cold water and drain well; be careful not to tear the leaves.

Take about half the spinach and lay it neatly and evenly in a bamboo rolling mat, making a thick roll near the front edge. Roll it up firmly, then leave to rest in the mat for a few minutes before gently unrolling to make a long cylinder of spinach. With a sharp knife cut the roll into 1-inch slices. Repeat with the remaining spinach.

TO SERVE Toast the sesame seeds (see page 28), spread them in a bowl, then dip one end of each spinach roll into the seeds. Stand 3 or 4 rolls upright in small deep bowls of a contrasting color and serve with a little soy sauce.

Spinach rolls: roll the spinach in a bamboo rolling mat, cut into even slices, then dip into sesame seeds.

Spinach "Asparagus" with Walnut Dressing

HORENSO KURUMI-AE

■

In Zen temple cookery, nothing is wasted. The bottom inch or so of pink spinach stalks, surprisingly, turns out to taste like asparagus, and is quite delicious served with a walnut dressing. The dressing, a variation on sesame dressing, can also be served with spinach leaves.

SERVES 4

*12-16 spinach stalks, joined together
  (see recipe on page 157)*

salt

WALNUT DRESSING

2 ounces shelled walnuts

2 teaspoons soy sauce

½ teaspoon sugar

4-6 teaspoons dashi (see page 22)

dash of sake (optional)

PREPARATION *Spinach:* Cut off the bottom 1-1½ inches of stalk and the pink, fleshy root of the spinach and trim the bottom and any brown or tough-looking parts. Wash very well; use a skewer to dislodge grit. Parboil in lightly salted water for 2 minutes, until tender, then drain. Leave small roots whole and slice large roots lengthways.

Walnut dressing: Grind the walnuts in a *suribachi;* you can also use an electric grinder, but be sure to leave the walnuts quite chunky. Stir in the other ingredients, adding enough dashi to give the consistency of peanut butter.

TO SERVE Put the spinach "asparagus" into 4 small deep bowls and top with the walnut dressing.

COOKING AT THE TABLE

Nabemono

Eating is very far from just a matter of filling the stomach in Japan. It is a time when people gather together, a time for sociability. One of the most sociable ways of eating is to put a pot in the middle of the table, simmering on a gas ring. As the assorted diners—be they guests or family members—chat, they also participate in the cooking process, filling the pot with raw ingredients and helping themselves when the food is cooked just to their taste.

One of the most famous of these sociable occasions is the daily meal of the sumo wrestlers. Chanko, the sumo wrestlers' stew, is the secret of their vast size; and to see these mountainous near-naked men piling meat and vegetables into a pot the size of a kitchen sink and downing bowl after bowl of the protein-rich stew is an unforgettable sight.

Many of these table-cooked dishes are rich in meat. Beef, in particular, forms the basis for two of the most well known, sukiyaki and shabu-shabu. Until little more than a hundred years ago, the Japanese were strictly prohibited as good Buddhists from eating meat. Then came the Meiji Restoration, in 1868, when the country was overwhelmed with a great influx of Westerners and Western ideas. Noticing that the Westerners were larger and stronger than the Japanese, the government decided that their meat-rich diet must be the cause of it. On New Year's Day 1872, the Emperor Meiji made a momentous announcement. "I will eat meat," he said; and from then on the Japanese added meat to their diet.

To cook at table, you will need certain pieces of equipment. The most important is a gas or electric burner which can be used on the table. On this you set a large and attractive flameproof casserole with a lid. In Japan earthenware and cast-iron are the most common. You will also need chopsticks for putting food in and out of the casserole and a ladle for dishing up the stock. Each person should have a dipping bowl for sauces and food. Provide about twice as many vegetables as meat or fish, and arrange the raw ingredients as appetizingly as possible on one or two large serving platters.

Sukiyaki

ILLUSTRATED ON PAGE 147

Sukiyaki is a wonderful stew of prime beef and vegetables, lightly cooked in a rich sauce, which, as the meal progresses, gradually becomes more and more flavorsome as it absorbs juices from the cooking foods. The word itself means "grilled on a ploughshare," and there are various theories as to its origin. One is that, when sukiyaki was first served, there was still quite a taboo against eating meat, and beef was cooked on a ploughshare to avoid polluting the household cooking pans. Another is that hunters and farmers far from home used to cook freshly caught meat on whatever implement was available—such as a ploughshare.

In its day, sukiyaki was a very fashionable dish. After the Emperor's famous declaration that he would eat meat, sukiyaki houses opened up all around Tokyo, where up-to-the-minute young men, who sported bowler hats, canes, and fob watches and wore overcoats over their traditional robes, used to gather to mingle chopsticks over this most new-fangled of foods.

To make sukiyaki, you will need beef sliced paper-thin. Ask your butcher to slice it for you on a bacon slicer. In Japan, sukiyaki is usually cooked in a special sukiyaki pan, a flat cast-iron pan rather like a frying pan (see page 34). An electric frying pan or a deep frying pan set on a burner will do very well.

The traditional accompaniment for sukiyaki is a raw egg. Just before eating, you break an egg into a bowl, beat it, and dip hot meat and vegetables into it; the egg cooks slightly from the heat of the food. If raw egg does not appeal, simply omit it and eat the sukiyaki with its flavorful sauce. The following quantities make quite a lot of sauce, which can be refrigerated and used again. If you don't like suet, use vegetable oil.

SERVES 4

1¼ pounds top-quality boneless beef, rump or sirloin, cut into paper-thin slices

8 fresh shiitake or other large flat mushrooms, wiped

2 thin leeks, washed and trimmed

1 onion, peeled

7 ounces shirataki noodles

8 ounces fresh tofu

4 ounces spinach or Chinese cabbage, washed and trimmed

beef suet

4 eggs (see page 31) (optional)

SAUCE

⅔ cup mirin

⅔ cup sake

⅔ cup soy sauce

1⅓ cups dashi (see page 22)

2 tablespoons sugar

PREPARATION *Beef:* Either buy ready-sliced beef or slice it yourself. To do so, semi-freeze it until it is firm and slice it very finely across the grain. Cut it into 1-inch strips.

Mushrooms: Cut off and discard the mushroom stalks; notch a decorative cross in each mushroom cap (see page 111).

Leeks: Cut the leeks on the diagonal into 1½-inch chunks.

Onion: Cut the onion into chunks.

Shirataki noodles: Parboil the shirataki for 1-2 minutes and drain.

Tofu: Cut the tofu into 1½-inch cubes.

Spinach: Leave spinach leaves whole. Cut Chinese cabbage into quarters, then across into slices.

Lay out the beef slices on one large platter and the vegetables on another.

Sauce: Put the mirin and sake in a small saucepan and boil for 2 minutes to reduce the alcohol. Add the soy sauce, dashi, and sugar and bring the sauce just to the boil to dissolve the sugar. Pour the completed sauce into a jug.

TO COOK AND SERVE Set up a sukiyaki pan or frying pan on a burner in the center of the table. Over medium heat, thoroughly grease the sides and bottom of the pan with suet. Put a few slices of beef into the pan to start off the cooking and quickly sear both sides, turning them with chopsticks. As soon as the meat changes color, pour in some sauce.

Provide each person with a small bowl for dipping and an egg, which they break into the bowl. When the meat is cooked (it will take no more than a minute), remove it, dip it in egg, and eat it. The egg cooks onto the hot food and adds to the richness of the flavor.

Next put in some vegetables, adding the harder vegetables—leeks, onion, Chinese cabbage if used—first. Then switch back to the meat, and follow this with more vegetables—mushrooms, shirataki, and tofu. Spinach needs the least cooking time and is always added last. Top up the sauce as you go along and continue to cook meat and vegetables alternately until everyone is satisfied. Be careful not to let the meat or vegetables overcook.

Shabu-Shabu

■

Along with sukiyaki, shabu-shabu is the most famous of the table-cooked dishes. It too consists of beef, in this case even thinner than for sukiyaki, held in the chopsticks and swished around in simmering broth, so that it makes a "shabu-shabu" sound. It is served with a couple of delectable sauces, one lemony, the other made with sesame.

SERVES 4

1¼ pounds top-quality boneless beef, rump or sirloin, cut into paper-thin slices

4 leaves Chinese cabbage, washed and patted dry

4 ounces spinach, washed and trimmed

2 medium carrots, peeled

8 fresh shiitake or other large flat mushrooms, wiped

2 thin leeks, washed and trimmed

8 ounces fresh tofu

Ponzu Sauce (see page 61)

parsley or watercress to garnish

SESAME SAUCE

⅔ cup white sesame seeds

6 tablespoons dashi (see page 22)

3 tablespoons dark soy sauce

1 tablespoon mirin

1½ teaspoons sugar

1 tablespoon sake

SEASONINGS

Red Maple Radish (see page 59)

2 green onions

4-inch piece dried kombu seaweed

PREPARATION *Beef:* Either buy ready-sliced beef or slice it yourself. To do so, semi-freeze the beef until it is firm and slice it very finely across the grain with a sharp knife. Cut it into 1-inch strips.

Chinese cabbage and spinach rolls: Parboil the Chinese cabbage leaves for 2-3 minutes until pliable, then drain and pat dry. Blanch the spinach in lightly salted water for 30 seconds to 1 minute until it turns bright green and begins to wilt. Drain and plunge into cold water. Drain again and make it into 2 rolls using a bamboo rolling mat (see page 158). Lay 2 Chinese cabbage leaves on the mat with the edges overlapping and the stalks pointing in opposite directions; put a spinach roll on top and roll it into a tight cylinder. Leave it in the mat for a few minutes, then unroll and cut across into 1-inch lengths. Repeat with the remaining Chinese cabbage leaves and spinach roll. Or, if all this seems like too much trouble, just use the leaves.

Carrots: Cut the carrots into flowers (see page 39 or use a cutter).

Mushrooms: Cut off and discard the mushroom stalks; notch a decorative cross in each mushroom cap (see page 111).

Leeks: Cut the leeks on the diagonal into 1½-inch chunks.

Tofu: Cut the tofu into 1½-inch cubes.

Arrange all these ingredients on 1 or 2 platters, grouping each type of ingredient together. Garnish with parsley or watercress.

Ponzu sauce: Make the ponzu sauce and put it in 4 small bowls for dipping.

Sesame sauce: Lightly toast the sesame seeds (see page 28), then grind until pasty in a *suribachi*, mortar and pestle, or electric grinder (you can also use commercially available tahini, sesame paste). Gradually blend in the remaining sauce ingredients, adding enough dashi to make a thin sauce. Pour the sesame sauce into 4 small dipping bowls.

Seasonings: Prepare the red maple radish and shape it into 4 mounds. Chop the green onions very finely, rinse in cold water, squeeze, and pat dry. Divide the seasonings also between 4 small bowls.

TO COOK AND SERVE Put a large flameproof casserole (traditionally a brass pot) on a burner in the center of the table and fill it three-quarters full of water. Wipe the kombu and score it a few times to help release the flavor, then add to the water and bring to the boil. Remove the kombu and turn down the heat so that the stock is simmering. It is now up to the guests to cook the meal.

First, mix the red maple radish into the ponzu sauce and a few green onion slices into either sauce. With chopsticks, pick up a slice of beef and swish it around in the stock for a few seconds, until it changes color, then dip it in one of the sauces and eat immediately. Put some of the vegetables into the stock to cook, beginning with the harder ones which need more time. Gradually the stock will absorb the flavor of the meat and vegetables.

When everyone has had enough, ladle the broth into bowls, sprinkle with a little salt and green onion, and serve as soup.

Fish and Vegetable Stew

CHIRINABE.

∎

This is a wonderfully rich casserole of fish, vegetables, and tofu, a sort of fish shabu-shabu. Best of all is to use fresh fish— and to use the whole thing, skin, bones, head, and all. In Japan the head is considered the best part of all, particularly the cheeks and the flesh around the eyes (and the eyes too). This recipe is excellent with any firm-fleshed white fish—rockfish, sea bass, hake, plaice, and haddock are all good.

SERVES 4

1½ pounds white fish (sea bass, hake, rockfish, plaice, or haddock)

4 leaves Chinese cabbage and 4 ounces spinach, made into 2 rolls (see page 158)

2 medium carrots, peeled

8 fresh shiitake or other large flat mushrooms, wiped

2 thin leeks, washed and trimmed

8 ounces fresh tofu

Ponzu Sauce (see page 61)

SEASONINGS

1 lemon

Red Maple Radish (see page 59)

2 green onions

2-inch piece fresh ginger root

4-inch piece dried kombu seaweed

PREPARATION *Fish:* Fillet and skin the fish, saving the bones, skin, and head for stock (or have your fish market do this for you). Cut the fish into 2-inch chunks. Refrigerate the cut fish until you are ready to use it.

Vegetables: Prepare the Chinese cabbage and spinach rolls (or simply use the leaves without rolling). Make the carrots into flowers (see page 39—or use a cutter). Cut off and discard the mushroom stalks; notch a decorative cross in each cap (see page 111). Slice the leeks on the diagonal into 1½-inch chunks. Cut the tofu into 1½-inch cubes.

Arrange all these ingredients on 1 or 2 large platters to look as attractive and appetizing as possible. Group each type of ingredient together and garnish with carrot flowers.

Ponzu sauce: Make the ponzu sauce and put it in 4 small bowls for dipping.

Seasonings: Cut the lemon into 4 wedges. Prepare the red maple radish and shape it into 4 mounds. Chop the green onions very finely, rinse in cold water, squeeze, and pat dry. Grate the ginger on a fine grater and shape it into 4 mounds. Divide these seasonings also among the 4 small bowls.

TO COOK AND SERVE Wipe the kombu and score it a few times to release the flavor. Put it into a large saucepan and add the fish bones, head, and skin. Fill the saucepan two-thirds full of water; there should be enough water to cover the bones. Bring the water to the boil and simmer for up to 20 minutes, skimming occasionally to remove scum.

Strain the stock into a large attractive flameproof casserole and continue to boil, uncovered, until the liquid is reduced to about 5 cups. Skim again.

If you have a burner for table-top cooking, take the casserole to the table at this stage and put it on the burner. Otherwise finish off the cooking in the kitchen, then carry the finished dish to the table.

First put the carrots into the simmering stock. When they are nearly done, add the mushrooms and leeks and cook for 3 minutes. Then add the tofu and cabbage and lastly the fish. Leave to simmer for 3-4 minutes, until the fish is done. Taste the stock and add salt if necessary.

The guests mix seasonings into the ponzu sauce according to taste, then dip the cooked food as it is ready into the sauce before eating. Serve rice and pickles to complete the meal.

Sumo Wrestlers' Stew

CHANKO-NABE

■

Chanko is the staple diet of the sumo wrestlers. Every day, while the senior wrestlers are resting after their 6-hour morning workout, the younger ones retire to the kitchen, to chop up meat or seafood and vegetables. The highest ranking wrestlers eat first. They sit cross-legged, naked except for the wide loincloth-like belts which they wear while they are training, and help themselves out of great simmering pots full of food.

Practically anything can go into a chanko stew. The only rule seems to be that it is based on either meat or fish but not usually both. Fortunately the cause of the sumo wrestlers' vast size is not the contents of the chanko but the amount that they eat—dieters have no need to worry!

This recipe is served during sumo tournaments and features chicken because four-legged animals (down on all fours) and fish (no hands or feet) might be bad luck. The quantities, as one might expect, are rather large; you may want to halve them.

SERVES 4

1 medium chicken

2-3 leeks, washed and trimmed

4 carrots, peeled

1 daikon radish, peeled

1 medium or large potato, peeled

salt

*10-12 shiitake mushrooms
(if using dry ones, soak in
warm water until soft)*

2 medium onions, peeled

1 medium cabbage, washed

1-2 cakes deep-fried tofu (aburage)
(optional)

½ cup soy sauce

½ cup mirin

½ teaspoon salt

PREPARATION Bone the chicken and cut the meat into chunks, 1½-2 inches, reserving the bones. Cut the leeks and 3 of the carrots into bite-sized pieces. Put the chicken bones, leeks, and carrots into a large saucepan, fill it with water, and bring to the boil. Turn the heat to medium–low and simmer, uncovered, for 3 hours to make stock, then strain.

Cut the daikon and potato into bite-sized pieces and parboil in lightly salted water in a separate pot; drain. Cut off and discard the mushroom stalks; cut the mushroom caps and the onion into quarters. Chop the cabbage into small pieces, and cut the remaining carrot and the deep-fried tofu (if used) into chunks.

TO COOK AND SERVE Put the chicken meat and all the vegetables except the daikon and potato into the stock pot, together with the soy sauce. Add the daikon and potato when the other vegetables are cooked. Season to taste with mirin and salt and simmer a few minutes more. Serve hot.

When the stew is finished, hungry wrestlers sometimes top up the remaining soup with cooked udon noodles.

Riverbank Oyster Casserole

KAKI DOTE-NABE

ILLUSTRATED ON PAGE 148

Oysters are rather commonplace in Japan and not at all a delicacy. The best ones come from Hiroshima on the Inland Sea. In North America, most of the West Coast oysters are actually descendents of the Japanese. Try the delicious little Kumamotos. Oysters and miso make a particularly delicious combination. In this dish the whole casserole is coated with a thick layer of miso, like the bank of a river, which is scraped little by little into the simmering stew, making it rich and flavorful.

SERVES 4

2-3 dozen oysters, removed from their shells (see page 31)

1 tablespoon salt

4 thin leeks, washed and trimmed

4 fresh shiitake mushrooms or 8 button mushrooms, wiped

¼ Chinese cabbage, washed

12 ounces fresh tofu, drained

2 medium carrots, peeled

6-inch piece dried kombu seaweed

5 cups dashi (see page 22)

MISO "RIVERBANK"

¼ cup white miso

¼ cup red miso

1 tablespoon mirin

a little cool dashi (see page 22)

PREPARATION *Oysters:* Rinse the oysters in water to which you have added the salt, then rinse them thoroughly in unsalted water and drain.

Vegetables: Slice the leeks on the diagonal into bite-sized pieces. Cut off and discard the mushroom stalks; notch a decorative cross in each mushroom cap (see page 111). Cut the Chinese cabbage across into 1½-inch chunks and the tofu into 1½-inch cubes. Cut the carrots into flowers (see page 39) or use a cutter.

Arrange all the ingredients attractively on 1 or 2 large platters, grouping each type of ingredient together, and garnish with carrot flowers.

Miso "riverbank": Mix together the 2 misos and the mirin, adding enough dashi to make a thick but spreadable paste. Spread the paste evenly around the inner walls of a flameproof casserole, to make a "bank" about ¼ inch thick. Put the casserole over a low flame to cook the miso a little.

TO COOK AND SERVE Score the kombu a few times to release the flavor, then put it into the casserole. Add the dashi and bring to the boil. Transfer the casserole to a burner in the center of the table and bring the dashi back to the boil.

The guests put oysters and vegetables into the simmering stock and help themselves to cooked food as it is ready. Replenish the casserole with oysters and vegetables, gradually scraping the miso into the stock to make a rich soup. At the end of the meal, ladle out the soup into bowls. Be careful not to overcook the oysters; they are ready when they swell and the edges curl.

Simmering Tofu

YUDOFU

■

Tofu is a homely food, but it is also a central part of Buddhist vegetarian cuisine. Several of the great Zen temples in Kyoto have restaurants on the grounds that specialize in simmering tofu, where you savor this most delicate of foods in the austere surroundings of the temple. This is one of the most aesthetic ways of serving tofu, cooked very simply and served with the most basic of seasonings to highlight the flavor.

SERVES 4

2 green onions

1-inch piece fresh ginger root

1 piece dried nori seaweed,
    3½ × 4 inches

Red Maple Radish (see page 59)

handful dried bonito flakes

1½ pounds fresh tofu

4-inch piece dried kombu seaweed

DIPPING SAUCE

1 cup dashi (see page 22)

½ cup soy sauce

¼ cup mirin

2 handfuls dried bonito flakes

PREPARATION *Seasonings:* Slice the green onions very finely, rinse in cold water, squeeze, and drain. Grate the ginger on a fine grater and shape it into 4 mounds. Toast the nori and cut it with scissors into thin strips. Put these and the red maple radish and bonito flakes in small bowls on the table.

Tofu: Cut the tofu into cubes, 1-1½ inches, and arrange on a platter.

Dipping sauce: Put the dashi, soy sauce, and mirin into a saucepan and bring to the boil. Throw in the bonito flakes just as the liquid comes to the boil, then turn off the heat and allow them to settle. Strain the sauce through muslin and keep it warm.

TO COOK AND SERVE Wipe the kombu and score it a few times to release the flavor. Put it into a large flameproof casserole and fill it two-thirds full of water. Bring it to a gentle simmer, then transfer it to a burner on the table. Put in some of the tofu and let it simmer just long enough to heat it through—tofu becomes tough if it is overcooked.

While the tofu is heating, serve each guest with a small bowl of warm dipping sauce, into which they mix seasonings to taste. As soon as the tofu is heated, lift it out with a slotted spoon and put it gently into the dipping bowls. Continue until all the tofu is cooked.

RICE

Gohanmono

Rice is the staple food of Japan, very much more so than wheat or bread is to us. At the end of every meal, no matter how vast and how many courses there have been, there is always a bowl of rice, white, pristine, and gleaming. Rice marks the end of the meal and it also represents food; in fact, the same word *gohan* means "rice" and "food." It is almost as if all the courses that precede it are nothing but a series of hors d'oeuvres, exquisite tastes that precede the real nourishment, the rice.

For the Japanese, rice has a strong symbolic significance. If you travel around Japan, it looks like a land of rice. Everywhere you go there are paddy fields, spread out across the plains and etched in terraces into the mountainsides. In the winter they are brown. In spring the farmers plant out the rice shoots and the paddies become a luxuriant shade of green. By autumn the rice has turned a wonderful shade of gold; then it is harvested and the fields are brown again.

Today rice is an uneconomical crop. The government provides large subsidies to the farmers and there is very heavy pressure from the United States to import American rice. But despite all this, the farmers are loathe to grow anything else. In some obscure way, rice represents the Japanese soul.

The rice eaten in Japan is the *japonica* variety, which is shorter, more glutinous, and more flavorful than the long-grain rice of the Chinese and East Indian cuisines. When Japanese rice is cooked, it coheres so that it is easy to eat with chopsticks. Virtually all the white rice sold at Japanese markets in America is California-grown *japonica,* now labeled "medium grain" but still commonly referred to as "short grain." The varietal designation "Calrose" means that it is *japonica* rice. Premium grades are labeled with trade names such as Nishiki and Kokuho Rose. And the designation "new crop" signifies that it was harvested early in the current growing year. In addition to Japanese grocery stores, some large supermarkets carry white medium-grain rice. In a pinch, you could serve white long-grain rice with a Japanese meal, but be sure to cook it with much more water.

Cooking Rice

■

Most homes in Japan serve rice for breakfast, lunch, and dinner. In almost every kitchen there is an electric rice cooker, which cooks the rice for you and keeps it warm, so that you can help yourself to a bowlful at any time of night or day.

In the absence of an electric rice cooker, the following method should produce perfect Japanese rice—white, fluffy, and slightly sticky. It is difficult to give an exact figure for the amount of water required; it depends on where and when the rice was harvested. (American and European rice, grown in dry fields, need more water than Asian rice, where the fields are flooded.) Package directions on California-grown rice say to use 1¼-1½ cups water for each cup rice and not to wash or soak the rice. This will produce a softer, more Western-style rice than the following traditional method.

The quantity of water in the following recipe is one that I have found usually works well—though, to repeat, it does depend very much on the particular rice that you are using. In order to conserve all the steam and moisture, put a clean tea towel under the saucepan lid; twist the ends up over the lid so that they don't catch fire. In theory you should never lift the saucepan lid; each time you lift it, precious steam will escape. To check whether the rice has come to the boil, tilt the lid very slightly, take a peep, and quickly replace it; do not lift it off fully. Once it is simmering, time it, but avoid lifting the lid and leave it tightly covered until you are ready to use it.

SERVES 4

1⅓ cups medium-grain white rice   *1½ cups water*

PREPARATION Washing the rice is an important part of the cooking process. Wash it at least 30 minutes before you start cooking. Put it into a large bowl, add lots of water, stir it around, and rub it with your hands so that the white starch comes out. Pour off the water and repeat, several times, until the water is clear. Then drain well and leave the rice in the colander for 30 minutes to 1 hour; or leave it to soak in the measured water.

TO COOK To cook the rice, choose a saucepan with a tight-fitting lid. It is a good idea to wrap a clean tea towel around the lid; this makes the fit tighter and also traps the steam.

Put the rice and the measured water in the saucepan, cover, and bring to the boil over high heat. Simmer for 5 minutes over medium heat; then turn the heat to very low and leave the rice to steam for 15 minutes. Finally turn off the heat but leave the rice tightly covered on the stove for another 15 minutes, to make it fluffy—this too is an essential part of the process.

Once the cooking process has begun, try not to lift the lid at all, as this lets precious steam escape.

TO SERVE Keep the rice covered until you are ready to use it. Dampen a wooden rice paddle or wooden spoon and fluff it before serving. Rice is usually served plain, accompanied with pickles.

Rice with Chicken

TORI NO TAKIKOMI GOHAN

Sometimes rice is simmered with other ingredients, to give it color and flavor. One of the most popular additions is chicken.

SERVES 4

1⅓ cups medium-grain white rice

4 ounces chicken breast, boned and skinned

2 tablespoons soy sauce

1½ tablespoons mirin

4 dried shiitake mushrooms, soaked in water until soft

1½ cups chicken stock or dashi (see page 22)

pinch salt

finely chopped parsley or 2 sprigs fresh coriander

PREPARATION Wash and drain the rice, then put it in water to soak for 1 hour. Cut the chicken into shreds and put it to marinate in the soy sauce and mirin for 20 minutes. Drain the mushrooms. Cut off and discard the mushroom stalks; slice the caps as finely as possible.

TO COOK Drain the chicken, reserving the soy sauce and mirin mixture and mix this with the chicken stock or dashi and salt. Cook the mushrooms in this mixture for 5 minutes, then drain, reserving the liquid.

Put the drained rice, chicken, and mushrooms into a heavy-bottomed saucepan. Measure out 1½ cups of the mushroom cooking liquid, check the taste, then pour it over the rice. Bring to the boil over high heat, stir, then cover tightly with a heavy lid wrapped in a tea towel and simmer over very low heat for 10 minutes. Remove from the heat and leave, still tightly covered, for 15 minutes to steam.

TO SERVE Mix the rice with a rice paddle and serve hot, garnished with finely chopped parsley or coriander. For added color, frozen mixed vegetables can be cooked separately and stirred into the rice before it is served.

Chestnut Rice

KURI GOHAN

■

This is one of the most delicious of the mixed rice dishes, and is redolent of autumn. The best flavor comes from fresh chestnuts, and it is worth the trouble of finding and peeling them; but to save time, you could use unsweetened bottled chestnuts (from Chinese and Japanese grocers) or canned instead.

SERVES 4

10 large fresh (or bottled) chestnuts

1⅓ cups medium-grain white rice

1 tablespoon soy sauce

1 tablespoon sake

¼ teaspoon salt

1½ cups water

black sesame seeds, toasted (see page 28)

PREPARATION Soak the chestnuts overnight. With a sharp knife, skin them and peel off the inner skin. Cut them into halves or thirds and put them to soak in fresh water for another half an hour. Bottled chestnuts only need to be cut into pieces.

Wash the rice carefully, drain, and put to soak in fresh water for 1 hour.

TO COOK Put the drained rice, chestnuts, soy sauce, sake, ¼ teaspoon salt, and the water into a heavy saucepan. Cover with a lid wrapped in a tea towel, bring to the boil, and simmer for 10 minutes. Remove from the heat and leave, still tightly covered, for another 15 minutes to steam.

TO SERVE Mix well and serve. Make sure that there are some chestnuts on the surface of the rice and sprinkle with sesame seeds mixed with a little salt. Chestnut rice looks particularly enticing in a small, deep, dark-colored bowl.

Mushroom Rice

SHIITAKE GOHAN

∎

The classiest version of mushroom rice is made with *matsutake* (botanically, *armillaria edodes*), a large flat wild mushroom which grows under pine trees and is held in Japan to be the most delicious mushroom of all. Certainly if cost makes it delicious it must be; it is undoubtedly the most expensive mushroom in the world. Besides shiitake, try mushroom rice with any variety of cultivated or wild mushrooms.

SERVES 4

1⅓ cups medium-grain white rice

6 fresh or dried shiitake mushrooms

1 small carrot, peeled

dashi (see page 22) or water

1 tablespoon soy sauce

1½ teaspoons sugar

1 tablespoon sake

pinch salt

PREPARATION Wash the rice, drain, and soak in fresh water for 1 hour. If using dried mushrooms, soak them in water for 30 minutes to soften them, then drain, reserving the water. Wipe fresh mushrooms. Cut off and discard the mushroom stalks; slice the caps finely. Shred the carrot.

Drain the rice and mix in the vegetables. Put into a large saucepan. Top up the reserved mushroom soaking water with water or dashi to make it 1½ cups or simply use dashi if you are using fresh mushrooms. Stir in the soy sauce, sugar, sake, and salt and pour over the rice.

TO COOK AND SERVE Cover the pan with a heavy lid wrapped in a tea towel and set aside for 10 minutes. Then bring to the boil, reduce the heat, and simmer over very low heat for 10 minutes. Remove from the heat and leave, still tightly covered, for 15 minutes to steam. Mix well and serve hot.

Five-Thing Rice

GOMOKU MESHI

■

The most complex of the mixed rice dishes is a colorful and tasty combination of rice and five other ingredients.

SERVES 4

1⅓ *cups medium-grain white rice*

2 *dried shiitake mushrooms,*
   soaked in water until soft

½ *medium carrot, peeled*

1 *ounce canned bamboo shoots*

½ *sheet deep-fried tofu* (aburage)

¼ *cake* konnyaku

1¼ *cups dashi (see page 22)*

1½ *tablespoons soy sauce*

¼ *teaspoon salt*

1 *teaspoon sugar*

1-2 *tablespoons mirin*

PREPARATION Wash the rice, drain, and soak in fresh water for 1 hour. Drain the mushrooms. Remove and discard the mushroom stalks; dice the caps finely. Cut the carrot into long thin strips. Rinse and dice the bamboo shoots. Rinse the deep-fried tofu in boiling water to remove oil and slice it finely. Sauté the *konnyaku* in a dry frying pan until it is dry and not shiny, then slice finely. All these ingredients should now be in fine strips roughly the same size.

Drain the rice and put it into a heavy saucepan. Mix in the vegetables, tofu, and *konnyaku*. Mix together the remaining ingredients, check the taste, and pour over the rice. Cover with a heavy lid with a tea towel under it and set aside for 10 minutes.

TO COOK AND SERVE Keeping the rice covered, bring it to the boil and simmer over very low heat for 10 minutes. Remove from the heat and leave, still tightly covered, for 15 minutes to steam. Mix well and serve immediately.

SUSHI

Sushi occupies a special place in Japanese cuisine. Only the simplest varieties are ever made at home. For the most part, sushi-making is considered a job best left to the professionals. Added to which, part of the joy of eating sushi is the ambience that goes with it.

In a way, sushi bars are rather like pubs—noisy friendly places, where chefs with white headbands keep up a stream of banter and chitchat while deftly slicing raw fish and pressing it onto balls of rice with deceptive ease. When you walk into a sushi bar, they greet you with a great yell of welcome. You sit down at the counter, admire the rows of gleaming raw fish in the glass case that stretches all along it and shout out your order to the chef, who prepares your sushi as you watch.

Sushi bars range from extremely grand and venerable establishments, where the same family has been producing sushi for generations, to the humblest conveyor-belt sushi shops. Here plates of sushi, literally on a conveyor belt, roll by in a never-ending stream. You help yourself to as many plates as you can eat and at the end of the meal the cashier simply counts up the empties and gives you the bill. Nowadays there is also modern sushi—California rolls, for example, filled with avocado—and designer sushi, in which each one is as small as a sugar cube, incorporating exotic ingredients like raw beef and served with French wine (Muscadet and Chablis go well with sushi, apparently). You can even send out for sushi.

One reason for the mystique of sushi is the length of time it takes to learn the sushi chef's trade. Beginners can expect a ten-year apprenticeship before they qualify as fully fledged chefs. For the first two years they do little more than wash down the floors, run errands, and, all importantly, observe the master at work. Next they learn to cook rice to exactly the right degree of firmness and are given the secret recipe for the particular vinegar-sugar mixture with which their shop flavors it. Then they learn to make rolled sushi and finally, after four years, are initiated into the secrets of cutting raw fish and turning it into artistic creations.

Despite all this, sushi is easy to make at home. Although your first attempts may lack the finesse of the professional chef, it is perfectly possible to make extremely attractive and tasty dishes, which are particularly good for parties. Sushi is always served with sake or green tea and red pickled ginger.

Sushi Rice

SUSHI MESHI

■

YIELDS ABOUT 3 CUPS SUSHI RICE

Aficionados say that the real test of a sushi chef is the flavor of the vinegared rice. In a sushi shop the first thing to order is the mild-flavored egg sushi, so that you can check the quality of the rice. The exact proportions of vinegar and sugar vary chef by chef and area by area. The further south you go in Japan, the sweeter they make their sushi.

Rice for sushi needs to be a little harder than usual so that it can absorb the vinegar flavoring without becoming sticky. To prepare sushi rice you will need a large bowl and a wooden spoon or rice paddle. Sushi chefs mix the rice and the vinegar flavoring in a shallow wooden tub. There is always an apprentice standing by to fan the rice while the chef mixes in the dressing; this cooling process ensures that each grain remains separate and the rice has a glossy sheen.

SERVES 4

1⅓ cups medium-grain rice
1½-1⅔ cups water
pinch salt

VINEGAR MIXTURE
2½-3 tablespoons rice vinegar
2-3 tablespoons sugar
1½ teaspoons salt

PREPARATION AND COOKING *Rice:* Wash the rice several times until the water comes out clear—scrub well with your hands, like scrubbing socks. Drain it and leave to soak in the measured water in a heavy saucepan for at least 30 minutes. Add the salt, cover with a clean tea towel stretched under a tight-fitting lid and bring to the boil, then simmer over very low heat for 15 minutes. Remove from the heat—do not remove the saucepan lid!—and leave the rice tightly covered for at least another 15 minutes to steam. (Keep it covered until you are ready to use it.) Meanwhile prepare the vinegar flavoring.

Vinegar mixture: Mix the vinegar, sugar, and salt in a small saucepan and heat until the sugar dissolves; do not boil. Leave the mixture to cool to room temperature.

Put the rice into a large bowl such as a mixing bowl and sprinkle about one-third of the vinegar mixture over it. Quickly and lightly cut and fold the rice with a wooden rice paddle or spoon, as if you are mixing egg whites into a soufflé mixture. Do not stir or beat the rice as this breaks the grains. After mixing, fan the rice to cool it (or, better still, have someone fan the rice as you toss it).

Repeat this process and check the rice; it should be sticky but not wet. Add the remaining third of the vinegar mixture little by little, stopping before the rice becomes gooey; you may not need to use all the vinegar mixture.

Cover the bowl with a damp tea towel and set aside until you are ready to use it. Sushi rice should be used within a few hours.

Sushi

NIGIRI ZUSHI

■

When we talk about "sushi," *nigiri zushi* is really what we mean —luscious slabs of raw fish pressed onto delicately flavored rice, with a dab of hot wasabi smeared between. *Nigiri zushi* (the words mean literally "squeezed sushi") originated as a specialty of Tokyo. It is called *Edo-mae zushi,* "in-front-of-Edo sushi," because the wonderfully fresh fish used to come straight from Tokyo Bay, in front of Edo, the pre-twentieth-century name for Tokyo.

Like sashimi, practically any really fresh fish in season makes delicious sushi. One of the best alternative fish for sushi is salmon, though in Japan salmon is never used.

Make sure that the fish for sushi is *really* fresh. Yesterday's fish will *not* do; check with your fish market first.

If you are buying a large fish like tuna, ask your fish market to cut you a piece along the fillet; a steak, cut across the grain, will not do. For small fish, a whole fillet or piece of fillet is perfect. For more on fish, see the Sashimi chapter (pages 50-61).

SERVES 4

1 recipe Sushi Rice (see pages 186-7)

1 teaspoon freshly made wasabi

*1 pound very fresh fillets raw fish,
    skinned (tuna, salmon, squid,
    sea bass, halibut, red or Tai snapper,
    porgy, bonito, mackerel)*

*4 uncooked prawns, with shell
    but without heads (optional)*

soy sauce

red pickled ginger

HAND VINEGAR

½ cup water

1 tablespoon rice vinegar

PREPARATION Prepare the sushi rice and set aside, covered with a damp tea towel, ready to use. Put the wasabi in a small bowl. Mix the water and vinegar in another small bowl; this is "hand vinegar" and is used to moisten your hands to prevent the rice from sticking to them.

With a very sharp knife, trim the fish fillets to make rectangular slabs, then cut into slices of ⅛–¼ inch (tuna can be slightly thicker).

Take each prawn, if using, and skewer it lengthways to make it straight. Boil them for about two minutes until they are pink, drain, and remove the skewer. Shell and devein, then neaten the neck and trim the tail. Make a slit down the length of the belly and gently open it out flat.

Put all the ingredients ready to hand and prepare an attractive serving dish to put the completed sushi onto.

TO ASSEMBLE Moisten your hands with the vinegar, pick up about 1–1½ table-spoons of sushi rice and shape it into a firm even oval, 1½ inches long (about the same size as the top joint of your thumb). Be careful not to overwork the rice. Eventually, when you become practiced, the shaping of the oval will be done entirely with one hand.

Holding the rice in the palm of one hand, lay a slice of fish across the fingers of the other. With the forefinger of your first hand, quickly smear the fish with a dab of wasabi (too little wasabi is always preferable to too much!), then press the rice gently onto it, cupping your hand to mold the fish around the rice; the fish should overhang a little at each end. The whole process should be very quick. Turn the sushi the right way up and set it aside. Continue until you have used up all the ingredients.

TO SERVE Arrange the sushi on the serving dish; you can mix in some rolled sushi (see page 191) if you like. Provide each guest with soy sauce to dip and red pickled ginger to refresh the palate.

Sushi should be served immediately and does not keep overnight.

1 Sushi: holding a ball of rice in one hand, dab a slice of fish with wasabi.

2 Press the rice onto the fish.

3 Mold the fish around the rice.

Rolled Sushi

MAKI ZUSHI

Rolled sushi is one of the most attractive forms of sushi and also one of the easiest to make at home. It is rather like a sandwich—a roll of white rice, like a wheel, encircling a colorful core, which might include raw tuna or salmon, eel, cucumber, simmered vegetables like dried shiitake mushrooms, strips of dried gourd, or piquant Japanese pickles. The whole thing is encased in nori seaweed, which has a particularly delectable flavor of the sea.

In Japan, rolled sushi is on sale everywhere and, like a sandwich, people buy them for a snack or a quick lunch. There are sushi stands on the food floor of every department store and in shopping arcades, small sushi bars on every high street, and, if you have a craving for sushi at two in the morning, there is always some rather tired rolled sushi in the 24-hour supermarkets that dot Tokyo.

Rolled sushi comes in two varieties, thick and thin. For all rolled sushi recipes you will need a bamboo rolling mat; if you don't have one, try simply rolling sushi by hand or in a tea towel.

Thick Rolled Sushi

FUTO MAKI

■

Thick rolled sushi normally has 4 or 5 ingredients making up its core. The knack is to get the ingredients right in the middle of the rice, like the hub of a wheel. The preparations and assembly can be done well before the meal; do not cut the completed rolls but wrap them in plastic wrap and cut just before you are ready to serve. Like a sandwich, many ingredients go well in rolled sushi. Besides the following, try any of the ingredients listed under "Roll-Your-Own Sushi" (see page 198).

SERVES 4

1 recipe Sushi Rice (see pages 186-7)

6 dried shiitake mushrooms, soaked in water until soft

SIMMERING STOCK FOR MUSHROOMS

1/2 cup dashi (see page 22)

1 tablespoon soy sauce

1 teaspoon sugar

1 teaspoon mirin

1/2 ounce dried gourd strips (kampyo)

SIMMERING STOCK FOR GOURD STRIPS

1 1/4 cups dashi (see page 22)

2 tablespoons soy sauce

1 tablespoon sugar

1 tablespoon mirin

1 Rolled Omelet (see pages 91-3)

12 young leaves spinach

4 sheets dried nori seaweed, each 7 × 8 inches

hand vinegar (see page 188)

red pickled ginger

soy sauce

PREPARATION *Rice:* Make the sushi rice and set aside, covered with a damp tea towel, ready to use.

Mushrooms: Drain the mushrooms. Cut off and discard the stalks; slice the caps finely. Put them in a small saucepan with the simmering stock ingredients and simmer for 15 minutes, until the liquid is well reduced. Leave to cool in the stock, then drain them.

Gourd strips: Prepare the gourd strips by kneading in salt (see page 24), then rinse well and put into a small saucepan with the simmering ingredients. Cover and simmer for 20 minutes, until well flavored and soft. Leave to cool in the stock, then drain well.

Omelet: Prepare the omelet, pressing it into a neat rectangle. Allow it to cool, then cut it lengthways into slices and cut the slices lengthways again into long strips; each strip should be about 3/8 inch square in section.

Spinach: Blanch the spinach leaves for 30 seconds to 1 minute, until they turn bright green; refresh, drain, and pat dry.

Nori: Toast the nori by waving it over a hot flame for a few seconds. It will begin to change color and become fragrant.

TO ASSEMBLE Put all the ingredients ready to hand. Lay one sheet of nori on a bamboo rolling mat with the 8-inch edge at the front and the smooth side down. (The smooth side will be the outside of the roll, the rough side will be the inside.)

Wet your hands with water or hand vinegar and take a good handful of rice (about one-fourth of the rice prepared for this recipe). Cup the rice in your hands, press it into a ball so that the rice coheres firmly and press it evenly onto the front half of the nori (see illustration). Spread it firmly so that it reaches right to both sides; leave an edge of nori exposed at the front.

Make a groove along the center of the rice and lay a neat line of each ingredient—mushroom slices, 4 strips of gourd, 1-2 omelet strips laid end to end, spinach—along the groove.

Holding the ingredients in place with your fingers, roll firmly, using your thumbs to roll; the mat will help you make a firm and even roll. Seal the edge with a dab of vinegar and leave the roll to rest in the mat for a few minutes. You can use the mat to shape the roll into a rectangle if you like.

Gently unroll. Keeping the roll seam side downwards, wet a very sharp knife and quickly cut it in half, then cut each half into 4 so that you have a total of 8 slices.

Make 3 more rolls in the same way, until all the ingredients are used.

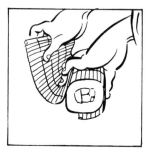

1 Thick rolled sushi: spread the rice onto the nori, and lay the ingredients in a line along the front.

2 Hold the ingredients in place with your fingers and roll firmly.

3 Seal the edge with vinegar, leave to rest for a few minutes, then gently unroll.

TO SERVE Arrange the sliced rolls on an attractive serving platter, garnish with pickled ginger, and serve immediately, with soy sauce to dip.

Another variation of rolled sushi uses dried gourd strips, *mitsuba* leaves (available in Japanese stores), rolled omelet, red pickled ginger, and freeze-dried tofu (*koya dofu*). This should be reconstituted in warm water for 5-10 minutes; squeeze well, then simmer for 5 minutes in dashi sweetened with a little sugar. Add a little salt and soy sauce and simmer over a very, very low heat for 20 minutes, then cut into strips as in the above recipe.

Thin Rolled Sushi

HOSO MAKI

■

Thin rolled sushi have a single ingredient at the core and are usually served in groups of 6. Besides cucumber and tuna (as in the following two recipes), other popular ingredients include gourd strips, *natto* fermented soybeans, and crunchy Japanese pickles, bright pink or yellow.

Kappa Rolls

KAPPA MAKI

■

Kappa rolls are actually cucumber rolls. They are named after the *kappa,* a legendary water sprite rather like a large frog, which lives in rivers and ponds and has the unpleasant habit of dragging horses, cows, and even children into the water. *Kappa* love cucumbers; and the best way to guard against them is to throw cucumbers carved with the names and ages of your family into the pond for them to eat.

SERVES 4

1 recipe Sushi Rice (see pages 186-7)

½ cucumber

salt

1 tablespoon sesame seeds

4 sheets dried nori seaweed, each 7 × 8 inches

hand vinegar (see page 188)

½ teaspoon freshly made wasabi

rice vinegar

red pickled ginger

soy sauce

PREPARATION Make the sushi rice and set aside, covered with a damp tea towel, ready to use. Deseed the cucumber and slice it into thin strips, about 4 inches long. Soak in lightly salted water for 20-30 minutes, then gently squeeze, rinse, and pat dry on paper toweling. Lightly toast the sesame seeds (see page 28). Toast the nori seaweed (see page 26) and cut each sheet in half with scissors.

TO ASSEMBLE AND SERVE Lay a half sheet of nori widthways on a bamboo rolling mat, smooth side down. Wet your hands with water or hand vinegar, pick up a handful of rice (about one-fifth of the rice prepared for this recipe), and press it into a ball so that the rice coheres. Spread it firmly over the front half of the nori (see illustration). Spread it evenly right to the edges, leaving an edge of nori free at the front to help begin the rolling.

Make a groove along the center of the rice and spread a thin line of wasabi along it. Lay strips of cucumber along the groove.

Gently but firmly roll the seaweed up to form a long thin cylinder and seal the edge of the nori with a little rice vinegar. Leave the roll to rest with the sealed edge downward and make 3 more rolls in the same way. Make 4 more rolls omitting the wasabi and sprinkling the cucumber with toasted sesame seeds before rolling.

Wet a sharp knife and cut each roll in half, then cut each half into 3 slices. Arrange the sliced kappa rolls on a serving dish and garnish with a little red pickled ginger. Serve with soy sauce.

Rolled Tuna Sushi

TEKKA MAKI

■

Very fresh raw tuna makes this one of the most popular sushi rolls.

SERVES 4

1 recipe Sushi Rice (see pages 186-7)

6-8 ounces very fresh lean tuna fillet, skinned

4 sheets dried nori seaweed, each 7 × 8 inches

hand vinegar (see page 188)

½ teaspoon freshly made wasabi

rice vinegar

red pickled ginger

soy sauce

PREPARATION Make the sushi rice and set aside, covered with a damp tea towel, ready to use. Cut the tuna into ½-inch slices, then cut each slice into ½-inch strips. Toast the nori (see page 26) and cut each sheet in half with scissors.

TO ASSEMBLE AND SERVE Lay a half sheet of nori widthways on a bamboo rolling mat, smooth side down. Wet your hands with water or hand vinegar, pick up a handful of rice (about one-eighth of the rice prepared for this recipe), press it into a ball so that the rice coheres, and spread it firmly over the front half of the nori. Spread it evenly right to the edges, leaving an edge of nori free at the front to help begin the rolling.

Make a groove along the center of the rice and spread a thin line of wasabi along it. Lay strips of tuna end to end along the groove and cut the last strip even with the edge of the nori.

Gently but firmly roll the seaweed up to form a long thin cylinder and seal the edge of the nori with a little rice vinegar. Leave the roll to rest with the sealed edge downward. With the remaining ingredients, make 7 more rolls in the same way.

Wet a sharp knife and cut each roll in half, then cut each half into 3 slices. Arrange the sliced tuna rolls on a serving dish and garnish with a little red pickled ginger. Serve with soy sauce.

Roll-Your-Own Sushi

TEMAKI ZUSHI

◼

ILLUSTRATED ON PAGE 150

This is sushi as pure fun, and wonderful party food. You, the host, provide a tub of rice, a plate of wispy nori seaweed and assorted fillings, all prepared. The guests then roll their own sushi.

The following quantities give enough rice for 4. Select 4 to 6 of the filling ingredients and multiply the quantities of rice and ingredients depending on the number of guests.

Shiso is a relative of mint; the leaves are sold in Japanese grocery stores and make a refreshing addition to sushi rolls.

SERVES 4

1 recipe Sushi Rice (see pages 186-7)

*8 sheets dried nori seaweed,
    each 7 × 8 inches*

FILLING INGREDIENTS

*8 ounces very fresh raw fish fillet
    (salmon, tuna, squid, etc.)*

8 medium uncooked prawns in shell

4 ounces smoked salmon slices

a little salmon or lumpfish caviar

*6 dried shiitake mushrooms,
    soaked in water until soft*

½ ounce dried gourd strips (kampyo)

1 Rolled Omelet (see pages 91-3)

¼ cucumber

*12 young leaves spinach or
    12 green beans*

½ ripe avocado

8 shiso leaves

garden cress or watercress

SEASONINGS

1 tablespoon freshly made wasabi

*sesame seeds, lightly toasted
    (see page 28)*

Japanese pickles

TO SERVE

red pickled ginger

soy sauce

PREPARATION *Rice:* Make the sushi rice and set aside, covered with a damp tea towel, ready to use.

Nori: Lightly toast the nori by waving it over a hot flame for a few seconds; it will begin to change color and become fragrant. With scissors, cut each sheet in half.

Fish: Cut the fish fillets into ½-inch slices, then cut the slices of fish into ½-inch strips.

Prawns: Shell and devein the prawns, leaving the tails intact. Thread each one onto a wooden skewer to make it straight. Drop them into boiling salted water, turn the heat to low and simmer for 2 minutes, until they are just opaque. Dunk immediately in cold water, drain, and pat dry. Finally gently twist out the sticks.

Salmon: Separate out thin slices of smoked salmon.

Shiitake mushrooms and gourd strips: Prepare the mushrooms and gourd strips and simmer in the simmering stock as for Thick Rolled Sushi (see page 192).

Omelet: Cut the rolled omelet into ½-inch slices, then cut the slices into ½-inch strips.

Cucumber: Prepare the cucumber as for Kappa Rolls (see pages 195-6).

Spinach or green beans: Trim the spinach or green beans, then blanch for 30 seconds to 1 minute, until just cooked, drain, refresh, and pat dry.

Avocado: Peel the avocado and cut it into long strips; squeeze a little lemon juice over if you like to avoid discoloration.

Shiso: Wash the *shiso* leaves and pat dry.

1 Roll-your-own sushi: roll the nori around a selection of ingredients to make an ice cream cone shape.

TO SERVE You should now have a selection of ingredients, all of which are more or less the same size. Arrange each in a small bowl on the table, together with bowls of the various seasonings. Pile the nori on a plate. Put the rice into a large bowl, provide a spoon for serving, and keep it covered with a damp tea towel.

To make rolled sushi, each person holds a piece of nori with the smooth side out, spoons a little rice into the center, adds a few other ingredients and seasoning, and rolls it all up; the final shape is rather like an ice cream cone (see illustration on page 199). Provide a bowl of red pickled ginger, and soy sauce to dip.

California Roll

CALIFORNIA MAKI

Some people say that the sushi in California is even better than in Japan, because there is such an extraordinarily wide range of fresh fish available. Certainly California has had an impact on Japan's sushi bars. Trendy Tokyo bars now offer California rolls, containing very unorthodox ingredients like avocado and caviar.

SERVES 4

½ recipe Sushi Rice (see pages 186-7)

4 sheets dried nori seaweed, each 7 × 8 inches

2 ripe avocados

½ cucumber, washed and patted dry

4 shiso leaves (optional)

1-2 tablespoons salmon caviar (lumpfish caviar is fine)

2 teaspoons freshly made wasabi

sesame seeds, lightly toasted (see page 28)

hand vinegar (see page 188)

red pickled ginger

soy sauce

PREPARATION Make the sushi rice and set aside, covered with a damp tea towel, ready to use. Lightly toast the nori seaweed by waving it over a hot flame for a few seconds; cut each sheet of nori in half. Peel and pit the avocados and cut them into long strips. Deseed the cucumber, cut it in half across, and slice it into long thin strips. If you are using *shiso* leaves, wash them and pat dry. Put the caviar, wasabi, and sesame seeds into small bowls ready to hand.

TO ASSEMBLE AND SERVE Lay 1 half sheet of nori smooth side down on a working surface. Wet your hands with water or hand vinegar, pick up a handful of rice (about ¼ cup), press it into a ball so that the rice coheres and spread it firmly over the left half of the nori. Smear a little wasabi in a diagonal line across the rice. On top of it lay a *shiso* leaf (if using) and some strips of cucumber and avocado. Spoon on a line of caviar, sprinkle over some sesame seeds, and roll the whole thing up to make a cone, rather like an ice cream cone. Continue in the same way until all the ingredients are used.

Serve with pickled ginger and soy sauce to dip.

Smoked Salmon
Flower Sushi

SAAMON HANA-ZUSHI

SERVES 4

½ recipe Sushi Rice (see pages 186-7)   *hand vinegar (see page 188)*

2 or 3 thin slices smoked salmon   *8 capers*

1-inch piece fresh ginger root, peeled   *soy sauce*

PREPARATION Make the sushi rice and set aside, covered with a damp tea towel, ready to use. Cut 32 small pieces of smoked salmon, each about 1½ inches square. Cut the ginger into fine threads, rinse, then squeeze well to drain.

TO ASSEMBLE AND SERVE Moisten your hands with water or hand vinegar. Take a scant ¼ cup of rice and shape it into a ball. Cut a 6-inch square of plastic wrap, aluminum foil, or muslin, and lay 4 slices of salmon in the middle with the inside corners overlapping, like the center and 4 petals of a flower. Put the ball of rice on top. Bring up the ends of the plastic wrap, foil, or muslin and twist them tightly to squeeze the salmon around the rice. Flatten it a little to make a flower shape and make a small indentation in the middle of the salmon. Finally, carefully remove the plastic wrap, foil, or muslin and put a caper in the indentation, like the center of the flower.

Continue in the same way to make 8 flower sushi in all. Serve 2 flower sushi per person, with a knob of ginger on the side. Provide a dipping bowl of soy sauce. Before eating, mix a little ginger into the soy sauce and use it to dip.

Another way to make smoked salmon sushi is to cut very narrow strips of smoked salmon, nori seaweed, and spinach. Lay them side by side diagonally on a piece of plastic wrap. Make an oval of rice (see page 189), put the oval across the slices, then wrap the plastic wrap round tightly. Take the plastic wrap off and repeat as required.

Scattered Sushi

CHIRASHI ZUSHI

▪

When sushi is served at home, it is most often served as scattered sushi—fish and vegetables artistically "scattered" on a bed of vinegared rice.

The following recipe is for scattered sushi as made in Osaka, with cooked fish and finely chopped vegetables. Tokyo-style scattered sushi uses slices of raw fish, cut as for *nigiri zushi* (see page 188), and chunks of rolled omelet. As with all sushi dishes, the topping ingredients can be varied according to taste and availability. Try any of the filling ingredients under Roll-Your-Own Sushi (see page 198).

SERVES 4

*1 recipe Sushi Rice
(see pages 186-7)*

*8 dried shiitake mushrooms,
soaked in water until soft*

½ ounce dried gourd strips (kampyo)

SIMMERING STOCK FOR
MUSHROOMS AND GOURD STRIPS

1½ cups dashi (see page 22)

3 tablespoons soy sauce

¼ cup mirin

1 tablespoon sugar

16 medium-sized shrimp, in shell

*2 ounces snow peas or green beans,
topped and tailed, or shelled
fresh peas*

*1 sheet dried nori seaweed,
7 × 8 inches*

red pickled ginger

EGG STRANDS

1 egg (see page 31)

1 egg yolk

½ teaspoon sugar

salt

vegetable oil

PREPARATION *Rice:* Make the sushi rice and set it aside under a damp tea towel.

Mushrooms and gourd strips: Drain the mushrooms. Cut off and discard the mushroom stalks. Knead the gourd with salt to soften (see page 24) and soak in water to cover for 15 minutes, then rinse well and drain. Put the simmering stock ingredients into a saucepan and simmer the mushrooms and gourd together, covered, for 20 minutes, until they are soft and well-flavored. Leave to cool in the cooking liquid. Drain, reserving the cooking liquid. Slice the mushroom caps and cut the gourd into small shreds.

Shrimp: Shell and devein the shrimp. Drop them into boiling, salted water, turn the heat to low and simmer for 2 minutes, until they are pink and opaque. Dunk immediately in cold water, drain, and pat dry.

Egg strands: Beat the egg and egg yolk together in a jug and add the sugar and a pinch of salt. Brush a small frying pan with oil and heat over medium heat. When the pan is hot, pour in just enough egg to coat the surface in a thin, even layer. When the edges begin to curl and the surface is dry, shake the pan and lift out the omelet. It should still be yellow, soft, and moist, not at all browned. Continue with the remaining egg mixture. When the omelets are cool, roll them up and slice very finely to make thin strands. Shake them loose to stop them from sticking together.

Snow peas, green beans, or peas: Parboil the vegetables for 1-2 minutes. Remove from the heat and rinse in cold water while the vegetables are still bright green, then drain and pat dry.

Nori: Toast the nori lightly by waving it over a flame (see page 26). Fold it lengthways in half and half again, then cut it with scissors into thin strips.

Ginger: Take a handful of red pickled ginger, drain it, and cut into threads.

TO ASSEMBLE AND SERVE Put aside half the mushroom slices, choosing the longest ones to use as topping. Chop the remaining slices coarsely. Put the sushi rice into a large mixing bowl and mix in the chopped mushroom and gourd strips. Add a little simmering stock to moisten and flavor the rice. Put the rice into a large dish. Smooth the surface and arrange the mushroom slices, shrimp, and peas or beans on top. Scatter with egg strands, threads of nori, and ginger.

Inari Sushi

INARI ZUSHI

■

Inari Zushi is small sacks of golden deep-fried tofu (*aburage*) stuffed with sushi rice. Like rolled sushi, it is a very popular snack food, served at parties and picnics or as part of a packed lunch, and is to be found in the most out-of-the-way village shops. It is named after Inari, the rice god, for a rather convoluted reason. Inari's servant is the fox, who has a reputation in Japanese folklore for being wily. And foxes are said to be particularly partial to deep-fried tofu.

Sheets of deep-fried tofu are sold fresh or frozen in Japanese grocery shops in packs of three. Thaw before using. The following recipe uses plain rice. You can also make *inari zushi* using rice flavored as for Scattered Sushi (see page 203).

SERVES 4

1 recipe Sushi Rice (see pages 186-7)	SIMMERING INGREDIENTS FOR DEEP-FRIED TOFU
hand vinegar (see page 188)	3 cups dashi (see page 22)
sesame seeds, toasted (see page 28)	¼ cup light soy sauce
6 sheets deep-fried tofu (aburage)	3 tablespoons sugar
	2 tablespoons mirin

PREPARATION Make the sushi rice and set aside, covered with a damp tea towel, ready to use. Cut the deep-fried tofu sheets in half and gently ease them open to make pouches. Put them into a bowl and douse them with boiling water to rinse off some of the oil, then drain. Put the simmering ingredients into a saucepan, add the deep-fried tofu pouches, and simmer for 15 minutes, until the simmering stock is reduced and the pouches are well flavored.

Leave to cool in the simmering stock, then drain and squeeze well until no more liquid comes out. Be careful; the bags are very soft and break easily.

TO ASSEMBLE AND SERVE Wet your hands with water or hand vinegar, pick up a ball of rice (about ¼ cup) and press it into an oval. Open one of the tofu pouches and gently insert the rice ball. Then fold the edges of the pouch over to enclose the rice, rather like closing an envelope.

Alternatively, use only 3 sheets deep-fried tofu to make 6 pouches; use ½ cup rice per pouch. Fill each pouch to the brim with rice and scatter toasted sesame seeds on top.

Silk Square Sushi

CHAKIN ZUSHI

ILLUSTRATED ON PAGE 150

It is well worth the trouble to make this particularly pretty and decorative variety of sushi—vinegared rice colored with red ginger and green peas, wrapped in a thin yellow omelet.

For a richer version, mix sesame seeds or peas into the prepared sushi rice, or use flavored rice.

SERVES 4

*1 recipe Sushi Rice
    (see pages 186-7)*

*a few strands red pickled ginger,
    about ¼ ounce*

¼ cup shelled peas, fresh or frozen

*1½ ounces dried gourd strips
    (kampyo)*

salt

"SILK SQUARE" EGG WRAPPERS

4 eggs

2 egg yolks

1 teaspoon sugar

*½ teaspoon potato starch
    (katakuriko) or cornstarch,
    dissolved in a little water*

pinch salt

vegetable oil

PREPARATION AND COOKING Make the sushi rice and set aside, covered with a damp tea towel, ready to use. Slice the pickled ginger into threads. Cook the peas for no more than 2 or 3 minutes, until they are bright green. Measure out and cut off 8 strips of gourd ribbon, each 12 inches long. Knead the ribbon with salt (see page 24), then put it into water to cover and set aside for at least 20 minutes to soften. Rinse very well before using.

"Silk square" egg wrappers: Put the eggs and egg yolks into a jug and beat well. Stir in the sugar, potato starch or cornstarch, and salt.

Brush an 8-9 inch frying pan with a very little oil and heat over medium heat. When it is hot, pour in just enough egg to coat the pan in a thin even layer. As soon as the edges begin to curl and the surface is nearly dry, shake the pan and lift out the omelet with a pancake turner or tilt the pan and slide the omelet onto a plate. It should be soft and yellow and not brown, and can still be moist on top. Lay it flat to cool, spreading it gently if necessary.

Oil the pan again and continue until all the egg mixture is used. The quantities given should make 7-8 omelets.

TO ASSEMBLE AND SERVE Gently take 1 egg wrapper and lay it on a working surface. Beware—egg wrappers are very delicate and tear easily! Have the strips of gourd ribbon ready to hand.

With wet hands take a handful (about ⅓ cup) of sushi rice and press it quickly into a ball. Put it in the middle of the egg wrapper and gently gather the wrapper around the rice; the rice will still be visible at the top. Tie the egg in place with a gourd ribbon and knot it securely, then fold the wrapper back over the ribbon; trim the ends of the gourd. Press the rice to smooth it and arrange threads of pickled ginger and a few peas on top as decoration. Use the remaining wrappers and rice to make 6 or 7 more sushi in the same way.

Serve 2 silk square sushi, garnished with a mound of red pickled ginger, on a pretty plate as a small dish in a Japanese meal or as part of a sushi dinner; silk square sushi also makes an attractive side dish as part of a Western meal.

NOODLES

Menrui

Noodles are nearly as popular as rice in Japan. If you are driving through the most remote and wild part of the country and come across a small house by the wayside with nothing around for miles except hills, trees, and rice fields, the odds are that it will be a noodle shop.

Noodles come in all kinds of shapes and sizes. The most common are soba buckwheat noodles, brown with a square cross-section; udon, fat white wheat noodles; and somen, thin white wheat noodles, which are often served chilled in summer. Noodles are always served quite simply, either in a broth or with a dipping sauce, with a couple of vegetables or prawns on top, so that the emphasis is on the flavor of the noodles themselves rather than the sauces that go with them.

As for noodle shops, they are usually quite modest affairs. At one end of the scale there are the noodle stalls on station platforms, where you can bolt down a bowl of noodles on the run as your train is pulling in. There are also plenty of small noodle shops where you perch on a stool at the counter and chat with the chef, like the one immortalized in the film *Tampopo.* At the other end of the scale, there are grand noodle establishments that have been purveying noodles, usually soba, for generations. Here you can watch the chef deftly rolling out a great sheet of buckwheat paste, then skillfully slicing it into fine brown noodles. At places like these, the exact ingredients of the broth and dipping sauce are a closely guarded secret.

Noodles are a good example of the way in which Japanese cuisine reflects the seasons and the locality. In summer the favorite dish is chilled somen noodles, while in winter noodles are served hot. Soba is a great Tokyo food (buckwheat grows well in the colder northern parts of the country), while udon is popular in Osaka and the south. Every New Year's Eve, as the bells strike midnight, everyone downs a bowl of *toshikoshi* soba, "passing-of-the-year soba." The long strands of soba represent long life for the coming year.

The etiquette of noodle-eating is to eat them so hot that you have to suck in a little air to cool them down, which results in a slurping noise. If you don't slurp, people assume you haven't enjoyed your noodles!

In most of the following recipes, either soba or udon noodles can be used.

Cooking Noodles

■

There is a set way of cooking noodles in Japan. They should always be *al dente,* cooked to the core but still quite firm. In noodle shops they are cooked in huge batches and reheated as needed; the chef puts a portion of noodles into a deep bamboo colander and dunks it into boiling water before serving. The cooking water from fresh soba is almost like a broth, milky white with all the starch. It is usually saved and offered to guests to mix with their dipping sauce and drink after the meal.

Allow 3-4 ounces noodles per person.

SERVES 4

12-14 ounces udon or soba noodles,
   fresh or dried

Like all pasta, Japanese noodles need to be cooked in plenty of boiling water in a large saucepan.

Bring a large pan of water to a rolling boil. Gradually put in the noodles, stirring to stop them from sticking. Bring the water back to the boil, then when it starts to rise and foam, pour in a cupful of cold water to cool the outside of the noodles to the same temperature as the inside, so that they cook evenly. Repeat this process 2 or 3 times, so that the noodles cook for 4-5 minutes in all (the exact cooking time depends on the noodles). Taste and check that they are *al dente,* then drain.

Rinse in a bowlful of cold water under a running tap, rubbing the noodles to get rid of the starch. Just before serving, put the noodles in a strainer and immerse them in boiling water to reheat.

Basic Broth and Dipping Sauce for Noodles

■

Noodles are served hot in a broth or cold with a dipping sauce. They can both be made up to a week beforehand.

Basic Flavoring

TARE NO MOTO

■

SERVES 4

½ cup soy sauce

½ cup mirin

2 tablespoons light brown sugar

PREPARATION AND COOKING Put the soy sauce and mirin in a small saucepan and heat over medium heat. When the mixture begins to foam, add the sugar and lower the heat, stirring continuously. Bring the mixture just to the boil, then take it off the heat and set it aside, uncovered, to cool. Once it has cooled, put it in a jar and store, covered, in the refrigerator for at least 12 hours. Use within 7 days.

Broth

KAKE-JIRU

■

To make soup stock for noodles, dilute the basic flavoring with 5 parts dashi (see page 22) to 1 part flavoring.

Dipping Sauce

TSUKE-JIRU

■

To make dipping sauce, dilute in the proportion 3 parts dashi (see page 22) to 1 part flavoring.

Winter Noodle Dishes

■

Noodles in Hot Broth

KAKE UDON / KAKE SOBA

■

This is the very simplest winter noodle recipe and therefore, according to many connoisseurs, the best.

SERVES 4

12-14 ounces udon or soba noodles   *4 green onions, washed and trimmed*

5-7 cups noodle broth (see page 211)   *seven spice pepper*

PREPARATION Cook the noodles (see page 210) and set aside. Prepare the noodle broth and bring it to a simmer. Slice the green onions very finely and rinse them in cold water, then squeeze and drain (the easiest way to do this is in a square of muslin).

TO ASSEMBLE AND SERVE Warm 4 deep bowls. Put the noodles in a strainer and immerse in boiling water for a few seconds to reheat. Divide them between the 4 bowls, ladle over the hot broth, garnish with a mound of green onion in the middle of the bowl, and serve. Pass seven spice pepper separately.

Fox Noodles

KITSUNE UDON

■

ILLUSTRATED ON PAGE 151

This is noodles served with a piece of deep-fried tofu (*aburage*) on top. According to folklore, the wily fox can't resist deep-fried tofu, which accounts for the name. Sheets of deep-fried tofu are sold frozen in packs of 3. Thaw before using.

SERVES 4

12-14 ounces udon noodles

2 sheets deep-fried tofu (aburage)

5-7 cups noodle broth (see page 211)

2 green onions, washed and trimmed

seven spice pepper

SIMMERING INGREDIENTS FOR DEEP-FRIED TOFU

1 cup dashi (see page 22)

2 tablespoons light soy sauce

1 tablespoon mirin

2 tablespoons sugar

PREPARATION *Noodles:* Cook the noodles (see page 210) and set aside.

Deep-fried tofu: Put the deep-fried tofu into a bowl and pour boiling water over it to rinse off the oil. Drain, pat dry, and cut each sheet in half crossways to make 2 squares. Put it into a saucepan with the simmering ingredients and simmer for 10 minutes until the tofu is well-flavored and most of the liquid is absorbed.

Prepare the noodle broth and bring it to a simmer. Slice the green onions very finely and rinse them in cold water, then squeeze and drain.

TO ASSEMBLE AND SERVE Warm 4 deep bowls. Put the noodles in a strainer and immerse in boiling water for a few seconds to reheat. Put the hot noodles into the bowls, add a square of deep-fried tofu to each bowl and ladle over the hot broth. Put a mound of chopped green onion on the side of each bowl and serve. Pass seven spice pepper separately.

Moon-Viewing Noodles

TSUKIMI UDON / TSUKIMI SOBA

◼

ILLUSTRATED ON PAGE 151

Despite the romantic name, moon-viewing noodles is a simple dish in which an egg yolk rests on each bowl of noodles, as golden as the full moon in autumn.

SERVES 4

12-14 ounces udon or soba noodles

5-7 cups noodle broth (see page 211)

4 green onions, washed and trimmed

1 piece dried nori seaweed, 3½ × 4 inches

4 eggs (see page 31)

PREPARATION Cook the noodles (see page 210) and set aside. Prepare the noodle broth and bring it to a simmer. Cut the green onions on the diagonal into 1-inch slices. Rinse them in cold water, then squeeze and drain. Lightly toast the nori seaweed (see page 26) and cut it with scissors in half lengthways, then across to make rectangles, 1 × 2 inches.

ASSEMBLE AND SERVE Warm 4 deep bowls. Put the noodles in a strainer and immerse in boiling water for a few seconds to reheat. Put the hot noodles into the bowls and ladle in the hot broth. With the back of a spoon, make a hollow in each bed of noodles and carefully break an egg into each hollow; be careful not to break the yolk. The heat of the broth will cook the egg a little. Garnish with green onion and nori and serve immediately.

Tempura Noodles

TEMPURA UDON / TEMPURA SOBA

■

Classic tempura noodles as served in noodle shops all over the country are made with giant king prawns, two per portion. But any kind of tempura is delicious with noodles. For tempura, see pages 109-114

SERVES 4

12-14 ounces udon or soba noodles

5-7 cups noodle broth (see page 211)

2 green onions, washed and trimmed

8-12 uncooked large prawns in shell

vegetable oil for deep-frying

sesame oil

flour for dusting ingredients

seven spice pepper

TEMPURA BATTER

1 egg yolk

1 cup ice water

1 cup all-purpose flour

salt

PREPARATION Cook the noodles (see page 210) and set aside. Prepare the noodle broth and bring it to a simmer. Slice the green onions very finely and rinse them in cold water, then squeeze and drain.

Prawns: Shell and devein the prawns, leaving the tails on. Rinse them in salted water, then in plain water. Score the belly a little to prevent them from curling up during deep-frying, then tap the back of each with the back of a knife blade.

Oil: Half fill a small saucepan with vegetable oil to a depth of 2-3 inches and add a little sesame oil. Heat slowly to 350°F.

Batter: Make the batter while the oil is heating. Mix the egg yolk and water very lightly with chopsticks; do not beat. Then add the flour all at once, plus a little salt, and mix in quickly to make a lumpy batter.

Arrange the prawns, batter, and a small bowl of extra flour beside the cooker, together with a rack or paper toweling for draining the cooked prawns.

TO COOK Check that the oil has reached 350°F. First flick a little batter into the oil; this will break up to make scraps that you use as a crust for the prawns. Take a prawn and dip it first into flour, then into batter. Resting it on a ladle, lower it into the oil. While the prawn cooks, pick up a ladleful of cooked batter scraps and roll the prawn around on the ladle so that it gets a thick coating. When it is cooked, remove it from the pan and drain head down. Continue until all the prawns are cooked. You will need to clear the pan and make fresh batter scraps from time to time during the cooking.

TO SERVE Put the sliced green onions into 4 small dishes. Warm 4 deep bowls. Put the noodles in a strainer and immerse in boiling water for a few seconds to reheat, then divide them between the bowls. Put 2 or 3 prawns onto each bowl of noodles and ladle over the hot broth. Serve each person with a bowl of noodles and a dish of green onions to use as a condiment. Pass seven spice pepper separately.

Summer Noodle Dishes

■

Noodles in a Basket

ZARU SOBA

■

In summer noodles are usually served chilled. Soba buckwheat noodles in particular are delicious and refreshing served extremely simply, with a tangy dipping sauce mixed with green onions and ginger. Serve in a shallow basket or on an ordinary plate.

SERVES 4

12-14 ounces soba noodles

2-4 cups noodle Dipping Sauce (see page 211)

1 piece dried nori seaweed, 3½ × 4 inches

4 green onions, washed and trimmed

1 teaspoon freshly made wasabi

PREPARATION Cook the noodles (see page 209) and rinse well in cold water; drain. Prepare the dipping sauce and put it in the refrigerator to chill. Lightly toast the nori (see page 26) and cut it with scissors into thin strips. Slice the green onions very finely and rinse them in cold water, then squeeze and drain.

TO ASSEMBLE AND SERVE Pour the dipping sauce into 4 small bowls, glasses, or cups. Put a knob of wasabi and a small mound of green onions into 4 small dishes. Set 1 bowl and 1 dish at each place. Divide the noodles between 4 serving containers, sprinkle nori over the top and serve immediately.

Mix wasabi and green onions to taste into the sauce and dip each mouthful of noodles into the sauce before you eat it.

Chilled Somen Noodles

HIYASHI SOMEN

More than any other dish, chilled somen are redolent of summer. They are the finest and most delicate of noodles, and are always served with ice cubes, sometimes plain or, as in the following recipe, with various different colored seafood and vegetables. Be careful not to overcook somen; they quickly become soft and limp. Somen noodles are sold in Japanese grocery stores in packets of various sizes, bound in bundles.

SERVES 4

*4 dried shiitake mushrooms,
  soaked in water until soft*

SIMMERING STOCK FOR MUSHROOMS

1 cup dashi (see page 22)

1 tablespoon soy sauce

1 tablespoon mirin

¼ small cucumber

salt

8 prawns in shell, raw or cooked

*12 snow peas, topped and tailed,
  or 12 sprigs watercress*

*egg strands made from 2 eggs
  and 2 yolks (see page 203)*

shreds lemon zest

4 green onions

1-inch piece fresh ginger root, peeled

*4 bundles somen noodles, total weight
  about 8 ounces*

DIPPING SAUCE

3 tablespoons mirin

3 tablespoons soy sauce

1 cup dashi (see page 22)

handful dried bonito flakes

½ teaspoon salt

PREPARATION *Mushrooms:* Drain, then cut off and discard the mushroom stalks; slice the caps very finely. Simmer in the simmering stock for 20 minutes, then set aside to cool in the stock. Drain before using.

Cucumber: Cut the cucumber into long thin strips. Soak in lightly salted water for 20 minutes, squeeze lightly, rinse, and drain.

Dipping sauce: Put the mirin into a small saucepan and bring to the boil. Add the soy sauce, dashi, bonito flakes, and salt and bring the sauce back to the boil, then strain it through a sieve and set it aside to cool.

Prawns: For raw prawns: drop the prawns into boiling water and simmer for 2-3 minutes, until firm and pink. Allow to cool, then shell and devein, leaving the tails intact. Simply shell cooked prawns.

Snow peas or watercress: Parboil for 1-2 minutes, just until it turns a bright green; then drain immediately and rinse under cold water to retain the color. Cut the snow peas on the diagonal into thin slices.

Egg strands: Make the egg strands.

Green onions and ginger: Slice the green onions very finely and rinse in cold water, then squeeze and drain. Grate the ginger finely (see page 24).

Noodles: Cut the binding tape and slide the noodles into boiling water, stirring gently to separate. Cook for just 1-1½ minutes; test and stop cooking as soon as they are soft. Drain in a colander under cold running water, rinsing well with your hands to remove starch. Drain again, cover with a damp tea towel, and set aside.

TO ASSEMBLE AND SERVE Somen looks most attractive served in small glass bowls, one per person. Lift the somen in small handfuls and divide between the bowls. Bury 2 or 3 ice cubes in each bowl. Arrange 2 prawns, a mushroom, some cucumber strips, and 3 snow peas or watercress sprigs on each bowl, keeping the ingredients separate; finally make a heap of egg strands in the middle.

Pour the dipping sauce into 4 glasses or very small bowls; float a few shreds of lemon zest on each bowl. Put a few green onion slices and a mound of ginger in 4 small dishes. Mix green onion slices and ginger into your dipping sauce to taste, and dip seafood, vegetables, and somen into the sauce before eating.

Mail-order Sources

The following companies fulfill mail-order requests for canned, bottled, and dried Japanese food products. Those marked with an asterisk will provide price lists or catalogs of their products.

*Anzen Pacific Imports
7750 N.E. 17th
P.O. Box 11407
Portland, OR 97211
(503) 283-1284
FAX (503) 283-0521

*JFC International Inc.
540 Forbes Boulevard
South San Francisco, CA 94080
(415) 871-1660
FAX (415) 952-3272

Katagiri
224 East 59th Street
New York, NY 10022
(212) 755-3566
FAX (212) 752-4197

G.T. Sakai & Company
1313 Broadway
Sacramento, CA 95818
(916) 446-7968
FAX (916) 446-2927

*Uwajimaya
519 6th Avenue South
Seattle, WA 98104
(206) 624-6248
FAX (206) 624-6915

Yoshinoya
36 Prospect Street
Cambridge, MA 02139
(617) 491-8221
FAX (617) 876-7657

Index

Author's Acknowledgments

Above all, I would like to thank Minoru Yoneda, chef extraordinaire and currently guiding light of Genji restaurant in Mayfair, London, who has been my mentor, friend, and guide in the art of Japanese cooking for many years. The beautiful food preparations in the photographs are his, as is the calligraphy.

Thanks also to Fiona Bennett for her expertise and enthusiasm; she fine-tuned many of the recipes and provided unflappable assistance backstage during the recording of the television series; to Alex Laird, for her friendship and her help in testing and tasting the recipes; to the many people who helped make both this book and the television series possible; and to Jill Coleridge for making it all run smoothly.